Goering Cross-Examined

Jacqueline George

Goering Cross-Examined
Copyright © 2014 by J.E. George
ISBN: 9781764215015
2nd edition: 2025

Cover design by Jacqueline George
All cover art and logo copyright © 2014 by J.E. George

ALL RIGHTS RESERVED: This literary work may not be reproduced or transmitted in any form or by any means, including electronic or photographic reproduction, in whole or in part, without express written permission.

All characters and events in this book are fictitious. Any resemblance to actual persons living or dead is strictly coincidental.

PUBLISHER
Q~Press Publishing

Notes

The transcripts of the Nuremberg trials are a record of a pivotal event in the twentieth century. They deal with great events and so their records deserve to be treated with respect. I have used them just as they were recorded, with the exception of correcting a few obvious typos e.g. inserting the apostrophe in "isnt", and formatting the names of the various speakers.

Other than that, the transcript is exactly as the stenographers wrote it, the exact words used in court. Of course, Goering and the defence lawyers spoke in German and so the transcript is a record of the simultaneous translation into English. The quality of the Tribunal translation services was recognized at the time as excellent, and Goering's words were rendered throughout by the best translator in the team.

I was brought up in England and naturally use the English style of spelling. The transcripts were prepared using the American spelling of the time, and I have left that alone. This means you will find both in the text, as with 'organisation' in my commentaries, and 'organization' in the transcripts; I hope this will not be an irritation.

I also had to chose between 'Goering' and more correct 'Göring'. I chose the former because that is how the name appears in the transcripts.

I have not given a list of the books I have consulted. There are more than enough books dealing with Goering and the Third Reich, and scholars can consult vast archives and libraries full of histories. Making sense of any part of this enormous wealth of written evidence is a job for professionals, and they can take care of themselves.

For the rest of us, it is hard to find serious books that give an overview of the trial and Goering's part in it. (I am not going to mention the films and television programmes!) I will recommend just two books:

~ *The Nuremberg Trial* by Ann Tusa and John Tusa. This is an account of the trial that is comprehensive and balanced, but manages to remain readable. If you want an unbiased introduction to the trial, this is it.

~ *Hermann Göring – Fighter Ace* by Peter Kilduff. A good account of

Goering's formative years.

There are so many books that cover Goering's years in power that we are spoilt for choice and even the smallest village library will have something to study. I hope this book will add to the existing record, and let readers see something of who the man really was.

Contents

Notes i

Foreword 1

The International Military Tribune at Nuremberg 3

Herman Goering - The Making of the Man 1893 -1918 7

Herman Goering - The Brutal Years 1918 -1946 13

The Prosecutors 19

The Cross Examination of Goering - 18th March 1946 - Morning 24

The Cross Examination of Goering - 18th March 1946 - Afternoon 34

The Cross Examination of Goering - 19th March 1946 - Afternoon 66

The Cross Examination of Goering - 20th March 1946 - Morning 79

The Cross Examination of Goering - 20th March 1946 - Afternoon 109

The Cross Examination of Goering - 20th March 1946 – Afternoon (continued) and 21st March 1946 – Morning & Afternoon 142

Goering's Final Statement - Morning Session – 31st August 1946 196

Verdict and Sentence - Morning Session – 1st October 1946 197

Epilogue – the Final Statement of Albert Speer 203

Foreword

The internet can be a dreadful snare for the unwary. You go online to search for, say, a holiday hotel in Europe and suddenly half the morning has slipped away and you are studying the trade in Baltic amber – something that had never crossed your mind before.

It was on one of those days that I chanced across the transcripts of the Nuremberg Trials, and they immediately swallowed me up.

I suppose what drew me in was the fact that this was history on a grand scale, a major world event, and it had happened so recently. Within our father's or grandfather's lives. History in our time, if you like.

What made me read more, and more widely, were the characters involved. I write novels. Characters are my stock in trade and without truly observed characters, no story will satisfy. Not even romantic ones like mine. Every good tale needs a villain or two, and here were villains galore.

I did not stay frivolous for long. The crimes the court was set up to examine were so horrifying, and on such a vast scale, that no-one can read about them without revulsion. Germany's Third Reich lasted for only twelve years, but in its short life it was responsible for so much death and destruction that even now, seventy-five years later, we are still feeling the effects.

After the war ended in Germany's defeat, the Allies faced the question of what to do with the high ranking Nazi prisoners they had caught. They also needed to consider what to do with Germany, and how to ensure it would not start yet another World War. They went some way to solving both of these problems by staging an open trial of the people responsible for the criminal past. The world and the German people would see just what had been done, and who bore direct responsibility for it.

The records of the trial are massive. Two hundred and eighteen days of formal proceedings and most of them make very dry reading. My attention was drawn to the records of the most senior Nazi, Goering – Field Marshall Hermann Wilhelm Göring – deputy Führer and second only to Adolf Hitler in the Nazi State hierarchy. Most of the defendants seemed cowed by their status but Goering took command of the situation and spoke confidently. His testimony leaves a chilling picture of a criminal regime.

I selected the records of Goering's cross-examination for this book. He did take the witness stand and testify on his own behalf but, as with any accused person, he gave a one-sided account of his life and actions. It is only under cross-examination that we can see the façade slip and unveil some of his real character.

That evidence is interesting by itself, but the dynamics of the courtroom brought more drama alive. The lead cross-examiner was an American, Associate Supreme Court Justice Robert Jackson. More questions were asked by a British barrister, Sir David Maxwell-Fyfe. The interaction of these three men – Goering, Jackson and Maxwell-Fyfe – makes a story that crackles with life and tension despite the dryness of the legal record.

Even though Goering is the centre of attention, I am not going to make judgements on him or his character. I am not a historian and plenty of much wiser heads than mine have covered that ground. The reader will have to make their own assessment from the record that follows. I can guarantee they will put this book down with a feeling of horror, and relief that Goering did not survive the trial.

The International Military Tribunal at Nuremberg

On the 8th May 1945, the Second World War in Europe came to an end. Unlike the First World War, this one had been genuinely of the twentieth century. Modern machinery, particularly the airplane, had spread the battlefield over the whole continent. Many soldiers had died but so had many millions of non-combatant civilians. In the last year and a half, Germany had borne the full force of Allied destructive power and now lay in ruins. With its cities and industrial economy destroyed, it was no longer capable of feeding its surviving citizens. There would be years of hardship before anything like normal life returned.

Psychologically, the war had brutalised all its European participants. They had become accustomed to violence and death entering their daily lives. Everyone had been touched by it, from peasant farmers who lost family or friends on the Army casualty lists to the desperately poor city dweller now living in a ruined cellar and wondering where their next meal would come from. Refugees thronged the roads, either returning home or fleeing from incoming regimes bent on revenge. Winter would come in a few months and everyone knew life would get harder.

It is difficult for the present day to truly picture the cold hopelessness of the times, particularly in Germany, but this was the context in which statesmen and generals had to work and build a new Europe.

The first order of business was the de-nazification of Germany, the rooting out of Nazi officialdom and the re-educating of party members. The Allies also had to comb through the prisoner of war camps, searching for war criminals.

At the same time, the military administration was consolidating into four zones, each under the control of one of the four major victorious powers – Russia, America, the United Kingdom and France.

Once it became clear that the Allies would defeat Germany but long before the war in Europe had actually ended, Allied leaders had already begun thinking about how they would deal with major war criminals. They knew, in general terms, the nature of crimes committed by German forces in occupied territories, and against the Jews and other groups within Germany. They understood that there could be no construction of a new European order until those crimes had been recognized and punished. For the first time, that punishment would not be of a defeated people but of the individuals responsible, all the way up the chain of command to the very top.

In October 1943, the Allies called on the fledgling United Nations to set up a War Crimes Commission.

At first, the leaders of the big three – Russia, America and the United Kingdom – did not approve of trying major war criminals in a court of law. Stalin preferred to solve the problem by shooting 50,000 of the most important Nazis, although he did jokingly offer Churchill a discount to 49,000 when he reacted with shock to the proposal. Churchill himself initially favoured a quick firing squad execution of any top Nazis caught, and Roosevelt seems to have been attracted to something similar.

It is to the lasting credit of the United States, and particularly Secretary for War Henry L. Stimson, that they used all their power and influence to persuade the Russian and British governments to set up the International Military Tribunal. At their Yalta conference in February 1945, the big three agreed that major war criminals would be tried in open court, given the opportunity to defend themselves, and either released as not guilty or punished appropriately.

Once the political decision had been taken, the lawyers could get down to work. As they sought to agree court procedures, their first hurdle was the fundamental difference between the Anglo-American common law system, and the more Napoleonic approach to law of the Russians, French and Germans. The first aims to uncover the truth by adversarial argument before a judge; the second is a more inquisitorial system with the bench taking responsibility for the investigation. Naturally, the first meetings of prosecution teams from the four powers (Russia, America, Britain and France) were difficult and laying down a mandate and procedures for the Tribunal did not come easily.

The second big difficulty lay in deciding exactly what crimes defendants should be charged with. The lawyers had no book of international rules to follow and instead relied on international agreements signed by the German state (which automatically had the force of law inside Germany). Reaching agreement on two charges was relatively easy – War Crimes, or breaking the laws and customs of war, and Crimes against Humanity or inhumane acts against any civilian population, such as enslavement or genocide.

Another count, Crimes against Peace or waging aggressive war, gave more trouble as the lawyers had no wish to create offences solely to prosecute the Nazi leadership. Everyone felt that marching into neighbouring countries and taking over by force was fundamentally wrong, and eventually agreed the legal foundation for the charge lay in international treaties previously signed by Germany.

The most problematic charge was that of conspiracy to wage war or commit war crimes. Conspiracy as a concept was familiar to British jurisprudence and Americans were well used to dealing with Mafia conspirators in their fight against organised crime. Continental lawyers found the idea much too slippery and it took some time to define the charge. It continued to cause argument throughout the trial.

As part of setting up the Tribunal, some possible defences were ruled out in advance. As a foundation, defendants and their lawyers would not be permitted to challenge the validity and authority of the Tribunal. The defence of 'I was only obeying orders' was also banned, as was *tu quoque* (legalese for 'you were doing it too').

Its legal foundation agreed, the Tribunal moved to Germany. It had been difficult to find a suitable location to hold proceedings as German cities had suffered terribly from bombing and invasion. The Russians felt strongly the Tribunal should make its home in Berlin – deep inside the Soviet occupied zone – but that had two disadvantages. Firstly, Berlin had been almost completely destroyed and secondly, no-one believed the Russians would treat Tribunal staff well. Within their zone of occupation food was in very short supply, and the Red Army was busy dismantling German industry and resources for transport back to the USSR.

On the other hand, the Americans were well known for having the most generous commissariat, and for being far better at solving supply problems. Life would undoubtedly be much more comfortable if the operating base of the Tribunal was within the American zone.

In the end, they selected Nuremberg because its Palace of Justice happened to be largely undamaged, and it had a spacious prison attached. It also had a symbolic resonance; the major Nazi rallies had been held in the city, and the anti-Semitic Nuremberg Laws had been introduced there.

The logistics of the trial were immense. The Americans especially had an army of lawyers and support staff to accommodate. The trial had to be conducted in four languages – English, French, Russian and German – and simultaneous interpretation was used for the very first time on a large scale. The defendants were prosecuted primarily from documents that they had signed themselves – the Nazis seem to have had a mania for recording meetings and conversations - and many of those records had been captured. If a document was to be used in court, it had first to be translated into all the official languages and enough copies produced for all the prosecution and defence lawyers – this in the days before simple office photocopiers. All of these support services had to work correctly all the time, and in a country so damaged by war that the population's major concern was simply finding enough to eat.

The war had ended on 8th May 1945. On the 19th October, a detailed indictment was handed to each defendant, and on 20th November the trial commenced. In a little over six months, an entire mechanism of international justice had been constructed and was ready to start work.

Could we do the same today? Certainly not. We have to remember that the men and women who set up the International Military Tribunal had been schooled in war. They had spent years fighting and struggling to get things done, because their survival demanded it. Their energy and can-do spirit are humbling.

Did they do a good job? Undoubtedly, considering the alternative to the Nuremberg process would have been to simply take the defendants out into the prison yard and shoot them.

Justice is never completely black and white but, considering the evidence produced, their eventual punishments seem to fit their crimes.

Herman Goering
The Making of the Man 1893 -1918

Hermann Wilhelm Goering was born in January 1893 at Rosenheim in Bavaria. His family belonged to the respectable middle class. His father, Heinrich Ernst, a retired cavalry officer, had made a career in the Imperial consular service and become the first Governor-General of South-West Africa – now known as Namibia.

Hermann Goering was the fourth of five children born to Heinrich's second wife, Franziska. At the time, Heinrich was serving as Consul-General in Haiti and Franziska returned to Germany for the birth. Baby Hermann was left with a family friend in Germany while his mother returned to Haiti – a practice that sounds very cold to modern ears, especially as she did not return for three years.

The family returned to retirement near Nuremberg where they were lent a house in a small castle called Veldenstein, the property of a wealthy friend, Dr Hermann Epenstein. Dr Epenstein was the young Hermann's godfather and had become an important influence on the family. While at Veldenstein, Hermann's mother lived as Epenstein's long-term mistress.

Much of what we know about Goering's childhood comes from Goering himself. While being held as a prisoner, he was interviewed by the Americans Dr Gustave Gilbert, psychologist, and Drs Douglas Kelley and Leon Goldensohn, psychiatrists. These were genuine interviews and not interrogations; Goering was able to relax and reflect on his early life.

Of course, he was speaking of a time more than forty years before and his stories were always more likely to be a reflection of how he viewed himself as a boy rather than a strictly factual account.

One example: in 1904, aged eleven, Goering was sent to a boarding school at Ansbach. Soon after his arrival, his class had to write an essay about the man they most admired. Goering greatly respected his godfather Epenstein, and chose to write his essay about him.

Unfortunately, although he had been brought up as a Catholic, Epenstein had some Jewish heritage and the headmaster knew about it. He berated Goering and punished him. Afterwards he was attacked by school-yard bullies and made to walk around wearing a sign saying, 'My godfather is a Jew'.

Very early next day, he packed his bags, smashed a violin he had been given as a gift, cut the strings on the school orchestra's other instruments and took a train home.

An alternative account of his departure from Ansbach is that he had been unhappy under the discipline there, sold his violin and bought a train ticket home with the money.

Which story is true? Perhaps that is not the right question; rather we should ask why he chose to portray himself as suffering for his 'Jewish' godfather.

From independent records and by his own admission, Goering was not a biddable child. He recounted that his mother once said, 'Hermann will be either a great man, or a great criminal'.

His parents decided to enroll him in a military cadet school in Karlsruhe.

Military discipline suited Goering very well. He thrived under it and when he graduated five years later, he entered the senior cadet school at Gross Lichterfelde near Berlin. The Prussian military caste had taken the place of his family, and in 1911 he graduated with the rank of Ensign, and was included in the *Selekta* group, roughly equivalent to graduating with honours. He chose to stay at Gross Lichterfelde for post-graduate studies and was commissioned as Leutnant in 1912.

His domestic arrangements changed around this time. His mother's place as Epenstein's mistress was taken by a much younger woman, and the family moved to Munich. Goering's father died there at the end of 1913.

In January 1914, Leutnant Goering reported for duty with the 4th Baden Infantry Regiment in Mulhausen, Elsass (now Mulhouse, Alsace).

He had hardly settled to his duties as a regimental officer when the First World War broke out. The next four years were probably the most important in forming Goering's character.

His war started with seven weeks of intense fighting around Mulhouse, in the Vosges mountains and on in the direction of Verdun. Goering proved to be a successful soldier and served as company commander. For this fighting he was awarded the Iron Cross 2nd Class. Suddenly, he was invalided to Freiburg suffering from severe rheumatoid arthritis in his knees. His future as an active soldier looked bleak.

Chance took a hand. An old friend was stationed nearby, as a trainee pilot at a flying school. His friend offered to take Goering on as his observer, a role in which stiff knees would be no hindrance. With a little help from his influential godfather, Goering was able to transfer from the infantry to the flying corps as an observer.

It is hard for us to imagine life as an airman in the First World War. The airplane itself was new, having changed from a plaything to a military machine in just a decade. Flying remained dangerous and attracted reckless young men.

Senior officers in the Army were not pilots, and the majority of them had never flown as passengers. At the beginning of the war, they had little feel for what airplanes could do. Day to day control of the air operations was left to the aircrew themselves, that is, to a group of highly motivated, self-confident young men who wanted to fly, hunt the enemy, and enjoy life.

Flying units quickly developed into close communities of fliers who lived, fought and relaxed together. The frightening experience of flying over enemy lines and braving the anti-aircraft artillery cemented these small bands of brothers and the men made friendships that endured over the years.

Aircrew saw themselves as an elite, and the general public agreed. Fliers were glamorous and, when the role of fighter pilot developed, the public treated them as stars.

The early airplanes were difficult to fly and unreliable. Many were lost to accidents during training and in normal operations although, as they flew quite slowly, a significant number of airmen survived to fly another day. At first, airmen were more likely to be killed by weather and accidents than enemy action.

The airplane had two military functions; to observe artillery fire and direct it onto the target, and to undertake photo-reconnaissance of the enemy's positions. The airplanes invariably had a crew of two, a pilot and an observer. In the German context, the observer was usually an officer and in charge of the airplane. The pilot might be an officer or a non-commissioned officer.

Goering threw himself into learning the technology of his new profession and soon gained a reputation as a hard-driving personality who would take risks to get the job done.

At this stage of the war, army staffs on both sides lacked confidence in the usefulness of airplanes, but that was to change rapidly. The artillery learned to use the information planes could give them and, at head quarters, mapping sections clamoured for more and more aerial photographs. Of course, if the two-seater photo-reconnaissance machine was useful for one side, it became obvious that they should prevent enemy two-seaters gaining the same access to their own rear areas. Single seat fighter aircraft were needed to secure the skies, and to escort photo-reconnaissance missions into enemy territory.

In mid-1915, fighter airplanes were reaching the front lines, and Goering was attracted to their independence and aggressive intent. He applied for pilot training and qualified at the end of September, but did not get his wish. He returned to two-seaters for the rest of the year, although he now flew as pilot.

In February 1916, the German army began an offensive at Verdun. The intention was to draw in French forces and grind them up in one of the most horrific battles of the war. Goering fought hard in this battle, flying both bombing runs and reconnaissance missions. While flying a two-seater, he at last achieved a cherished aim, and shot down an enemy airplane. He shot down a second victim next day.

Goering was finally able to graduate to single seat fighters in July 1916, after the Battle of Verdun and at the start of the British offensive on the Somme. He shot down a third victim at the end of July.

Goering was an energetic and aggressive pilot, sometimes flying up to nine sorties in a day, searching for the enemy and trying to engage him. The fighting was hard but frustrating, and Goering ended the year in hospital after being wounded in the hip in a dogfight.

1917 proved to be a good year for the German air force as new fighter models, particularly the Albatros DIII, gave them an advantage over their enemies. This was the period when Manfred von Richthoven – the Red Baron - established himself as an ace apart, and when the British lost a third of their aircrew in 'Bloody April'.

In May, Goering's energy and aggression were rewarded with the command of a squadron. Now he had the weight of the whole squadron on his shoulders, at a time when his British enemies were receiving new, technically advanced aircraft. The German air force never again achieved the technical advantage that they had held in early 1917, and they were slowly falling behind in aircraft numbers as well.

The pressure on the young men fighting the air war was immense. Patrols were short – sometimes less than an hour – but they flew and flew and flew again whenever the weather permitted. Aerial combat was particularly personal, with fighters shooting at each other from very close range. Opposing pilots could be clearly seen, and even recognized.

The strain of leaving their home base several times a day, never knowing if they would return alive and uninjured, exhausted the men. Goering seems to have been careful to take leave regularly to avoid burning out.

The hard fighting continued and by the end of 1917, Goering's total of enemy aircraft had reached sixteen.

The balance of forces in the war had changed. Russia had withdrawn after her revolution and Germany was no longer fighting a war on two fronts. She gathered her resources for a final assault in the West. If she were to succeed, she needed to do it before the newly belligerent Americans could arrive in force.

At this point, in April 1918, Manfred von Richthofen was shot down and killed. News of his death brought relief to Allied airmen as his aura of success had oppressed them. The news had an even greater impact on the other side of the lines. The loss of their greatest fighter ace shook civilian and soldier alike.

On the ground, the Germans reached a high point in April 1918. They were held and then relentlessly pushed back. In the air, the increasing numbers of enemy aircraft were beginning to tell.

Richthofen's famous 'Flying Circus' Jagdgeschwader I had a new leader, Wilhelm Reinhard. When he died in a flying accident shortly afterwards, this most prestigious command was given to Goering. It was a recognition of his aggressive leadership skills.

As control of the air passed slowly to the Allies, Goering fought hard, both in the air and with his superiors. He demanded, and generally received, the best for his airplanes and his men.

It was not enough. The tide had turned against Germany and the end of the war came in November. Goering stopped fighting with a personal tally of twenty-two victories.

For four hectic years, Goering had lived the war. He had flown and fought, been injured and survived, but in the end there was nothing to show for it. He had lost everything; his way of life, his close friends and his purpose. What would life hold for him now?

Herman Goering
The Brutal Years 1918 -1946

In December 1918, Goering attended a meeting of an officer's association and gave a short speech. In it, he decried the attitude of the general public to officers who had fought and died for their country. On behalf of the Army, he rejected any share of blame for the defeat. Instead he placed it on the shoulders of 'the ones who stabbed our glorious Army in the back, and who wanted nothing more than to enrich themselves at the expense of the real people'.

The stab-in-the-back legend was already well established, and given more credence as Germany itself had not been invaded. The civilian population had suffered shortages, but not military occupation. In his speech Goering looked forward to the day when the traitorous financiers and the politicians who had signed the Armistice would be finished and driven out of Germany. He ended by calling on his officer colleagues to 'prepare yourselves, arm yourselves and work towards that day'.

For the moment, these were nothing more than dreams. Goering had been a great man, an important part of the struggle for his country's life. Now, along with so many warriors on both sides, he found himself tossed aside. He had little money and his only marketable skill was his flying ability.

Goering drifted. First to Denmark where he tried barnstorming and then on to Sweden where he took a pilot's position with Svensk Lufttrafik, one of the many small airlines that mushroomed across Europe after the war.

Luck again favoured Goering. He had been hired by Count Eric von Rosen to fly him from Stockholm to his castle at Baven. Goering had to stay overnight because of bad weather, and here he met his future wife, Carin von Kantzow.

The years immediately after the war were turbulent times for Germany. There were deep divisions in society, with returned soldiers forming paramilitary organisations on the right, and militant workers on the left hopeful of achieving a socialist revolution. Goering watched the political tumult from the safety of Sweden and was not involved in the failed right-wing Kapp-Lüttwitz Putsch of 1920. However, he had not lost his interest in Germany's fate and in 1921 returned to study History and Political Science at Munich University. Carin followed him and they married in 1922.

In that year, Goering first heard Hitler speaking. He was immediately attracted to his revolutionary message and joined the Nazi Party. Hitler liked Goering and quickly recognised his energy and leadership ability. He later said 'I liked him. I made him the head of my SA (*Sturmabteilung*). He is the only one of its heads that ran the SA properly. I gave him a dishevelled rabble. In a very short time he had organised a division of 11,000 men.'

The Sturmabteilung (roughly, Storm Troopers) were a political militia formed by Hitler and the Nazi party. They were commonly referred to as the SA, or the Brownshirts. Their function was to protect the Nazi party and to deal with its enemies covertly, or openly when meetings were being held. Goering became their leader in 1922.

Goering was again living in interesting times. As Germany's new Weimar Republic struggled to create a modern economy, Hitler's revolutionary fervour and his new Nazi party offered a way forward that suited returned soldiers very well. He had a political philosophy, a vision for the future, and an organised force of men to support it. He believed he was strong enough to risk everything on a coup d'état.

Hitler chose to act in Munich and initiated the Beer Hall Putsch, named for the Bürgerbräukeller, a beer hall where the revolution started. It came close to succeeding, but the following morning the coup leaders were confronted by a force of State Police as they marched toward the Defence Ministry. Shooting started, sixteen Nazis were killed, and the rest were scattered. Goering was shot in the groin and severely wounded.

Helped by his wife, Goering escaped, first to Innsbruck where his wound was operated on, and then to Venice. As a wanted man, he could not return to Germany and the family moved back to Sweden.

During his initial stay in hospital, Goering had been given morphine to control the pain of his wound, and he became addicted. By the time he reached Sweden, his addiction had taken control. He was certified as a dangerous drug addict and hospitalised in a mental institution. The doctors there slowly weaned him from morphine. They seem to have used dihydrocodeine (a semi-synthetic opioid) in a similar way that methadone treatment is applied today for heroin addiction. Goering remained addicted to this less damaging substitute until he was imprisoned at Nuremberg.

In the meantime, Hitler had been arrested and sentenced to a very mild five years in prison. He had enough time to put his visions for the future down in an unreadable book (*Mein Kampf*) before he was released after serving only eight months of his sentence. He immediately began rebuilding his party.

After an amnesty was declared, Goering returned to Germany in 1927. He did not return to his position with the SA, but was elected to the Reichstag in 1928, one of only twelve Nazis. The next election, which took place in the hard times after the 1929 Wall Street Crash, returned one hundred and seven Nazis. Goering became President of the Reichstag in 1932, an office he retained even after the Reichstag ceased to function.

Hitler's final electoral victory came in 1933, when he was appointed Chancellor of Germany. Goering became Reich Commissioner of Aviation, and the Interior Minister for Prussia, where he set about founding the Gestapo.

Goering's first wife Carin had died of tuberculosis and heart problems in 1931. He remarried to Emmy Sonnemann, an actress, in 1935.

Hitler had begun to have severe doubts over the loyalty of the SA and its leader, Ernst Roehm. The SA had been formed to provide the street muscle through which the Nazis rose to power. Now they were the established government, the Nazis no longer needed the backing of SA thugs.

The SA had grown to number between two and three million, dwarfing the 100,000 strong official Army. They were demanding more and more say in government and even proposed to absorb the Army. Under Hitler's direction, Goering and Himmler, assisted by Heydrich, laid plans to use the SS (*Schutzstaffel* or Protection Squadron) to kill or arrest the leaders of the SA.

The purge began on 30th June 1934, and became known as The Night of the Long Knives. Roehm and the SA leadership were murdered, along with several other political opponents of the Nazis.

Goering's unquestioning support for Hitler, along with his energy and organisational skills, increasingly led Hitler to rely on him. He was secretly named as Hitler's successor in the event of Hitler's death or inability to govern. Shortly afterwards, he became commander-in-chief of the new German Air Force, the Luftwaffe, a position he held until 1945.

In September 1935, a seminal event in the development of Nazi power took place in Nuremberg. A Nazi party rally was held in conjunction with a session of the Reichstag. The infamous Nuremberg Laws were introduced at this time, aimed at isolating and disempowering the Jewish community. As President of the Reichstag, Goering presided over their introduction.

Hitler's plans demanded a militarily invincible Germany and in 1936 Goering was appointed Plenipotentiary of the Four Year Plan, an accelerated programme to rearm Germany and make it ready for war. Goering built an independent organisation to control the huge expenditures the Plan required. Both the Economics Ministry and the Reichsbank came under Goering's control, and the state budget began to accumulate large deficits.

Goering's influence spread far beyond his designated portfolios, and he was instrumental in the annexation of both Austria and Czechoslovakia in 1938 and 1939. The compliance of both these foreign governments was obtained by threats of force, delivered at least partly by Goering over the telephone.

By now, Europe was slipping towards war. Goering and other military leaders did not want war – yet. They felt they were not ready, but Hitler pushed forward and the Second World War in Europe started on 1st September 1939.

Initially, things went well and the results of Goering's re-armament efforts showed in the way German forces swept through a large part of Poland and Western Europe. After the fall of France, Hitler promoted Goering to the rank of Reich Marshal of the Greater German Reich (*Reichsmarschall des Grossdeutschen Reiches*). He became the highest ranking military official in the Reich and remained so until the end.

It was the zenith of his career and from that point military failure began to erode his status. Hitler blamed him loudly for defeat in the Battle of Britain, and for the bombing campaigns that the British and later the Americans were able to launch against the German homeland.

Goering promised an airborne operation to supply von Paulus' VIth Army during the siege of Stalingrad, but was unable to deliver more than a fraction of the supplies needed. The defeat at Stalingrad marked the turning point of the war on the Eastern Front, and Goering had failed again.

From now on, Goering was cut off from close contact with Hitler. He had been basking in the sun and acting as Hitler's most trusted deputy, but now he was banished from influence. He continued the routine duties of his position but spent more and more time at his palatial hunting lodge, Carinhall - named for his first wife and set in the state forest of Schorfheide, north east of Berlin. Here he indulged himself in partying, hunting, and his collection of art looted from all over Europe.

As the Third Reich collapsed, Goering sent a telegram to Berlin offering to act as Hitler's deputy. Deep in paranoia and with the Russians at his door, Hitler took this as an act of treason. Goering was stripped of all his offices and arrested.

The war ended with Goering in American custody. Although he apparently had some hope of immunity in return for cooperation, there was no question that he would not appear before the International Military Tribunal. He was by far the most important and most knowledgeable Nazi left alive and would be the centre-piece of the Nuremberg trials.

He was interrogated extensively, as were all the defendants, and interviewed by medical specialists. On a prison diet and without his addictive dihydrocodeine pills, he lost about 27 kilos (60 pounds) and began the trial looking fitter and more alert than he had for years.

He appears to have accepted from the start that he would not escape the death sentence. Most of the other defendants seem to have come to the same conclusion, but they were not as clear-eyed about it as Goering. He set himself the task of presenting the Third Reich in the most favourable light possible, and was determined that his co-defendants should do the same.

In his last months, Goering demonstrated some of his old energy, determination and leadership, dominating the other prisoners to the point where prison authorities decided to limit his access to them. Morning and evening meals were taken in their cells, but they did meet for lunch. Goering was forced to lunch alone, purely to limit his influence.

Unlike some of the others, Goering never repudiated Hitler and confirmed his support openly in court.

The newspapers and the public were initially very interested in the Nuremberg trials, both inside Germany and abroad. Interest waned as month followed month, but the world paid attention again when Goering finally took the stand in March. He spoke, almost without restraint for nearly three days, explaining the great events in which he had been involved, and generally portraying himself in a leading and favourable light.

When he had finished, it was the turn of the prosecutors to attack his story and attempt to bring truth out of the shadows.

The Prosecutors

Supreme Court Justice Jackson

Robert Houghwout Jackson, aged 53 in 1945, was a distinguished jurist. In spite of his young age, he had already achieved the pinnacle of an American lawyer's career, a Supreme Court appointment.

His road to success had not been easy. He remains the only Supreme Court justice who did not graduate from a law school but fought his way up from the position of junior clerk with the family law firm.

A peculiarity of the American legal system is the degree to which it is politicized. Parliaments around the world tend to be full of lawyers turned politician, but these people are mostly courtroom and corporate lawyers. The judiciary are treated as a class apart, tasked with making the impartial decisions at the heart of a legal system. American judges tend to be much closer to politics and in some cases are actually democratically elected to their positions.

Jackson, a Democrat, was politically active and became a friend of Franklin D. Roosevelt, Governor of New York and future President. Roosevelt gave him his first government appointment on a committee studying the state judicial system.

Once Roosevelt had reached the White House in 1933, he appointed Jackson as general counsel to the Internal Revenue Service. Jackson continued his career in a succession of appointments becoming the US Attorney General in 1940. He did not stay long in that position and was appointed as a Supreme Court justice in 1941. He was on track to become Chief Justice or even, in the opinion of Roosevelt, to make a run for the Presidency of the United States.

Jackson was never simply a practising lawyer, focused on winning cases and making a living. He had a strong belief in the law and its place in human society. He had a strong crusading streak and thought deeply about what he could contribute to the future. His future colleague at Nuremberg, Sir David Maxwell-Fyfe, later wrote of him 'In the truest sense, he was a romantic of the law. For him, the vocation of the lawyer left dull huckstering and pettifogging things. It caught the full wind of the traditions of natural justice, reason and human rights.'

Naturally, any deep thinker about future law would come to consider the place of law in regulating international relations. In particular, Jackson could not accept that the waging of an aggressive war should not be prosecuted as a major crime. International treaties already existed to give a framework of law betweens nations; all that was lacking was the will to enforce it. As he put it, 'It does not appear necessary to treat all wars as legal and just simply because we have no court to try the accused'.

When the President asked him to head the US Nuremberg prosecuting team, Jackson was inherently unable to refuse.

Jackson arrived in London in May 1945 with everything still to do. No book of procedures existed for the forthcoming trial. No list of defendants, not even an agreement over what exactly they would be charged with. Jackson did bring a burning ambition to set up and execute a trial process that would be both effective and moral, and that would provide an example to the future. He also felt it was given that, as the leader of the prosecuting team of the world's most powerful nation, he would be setting the agenda and bringing the project through to a conclusion.

His first meetings in London were with the British team. They liked their first impressions of him, but once they had begun work on his proposals, they were less enthusiastic. The British, who were mostly practicing courtroom lawyers, found his views to be abstract and impractical.

Jackson does not seem to have expected resistance from the other prosecuting teams. He believed they would soon come to agree that the American way of doing things was the best for everyone. He probably accepted in theory that other nation's citizens loved their own legal systems, but when he came face to face with top lawyers who did not automatically accept America's legal system as the best in the world, he seems to have become confused. The London meetings, between Russians, British, French and Americans, were always going to be difficult. Setting up the International Military Tribunal would not be simple.

The negotiations are a story of their own and it is to the credit of all concerned that the basic structure of the trial had been agreed by the time the Potsdam Conference between Truman, Stalin and Atlee (the new British Prime Minister) began on 11th July.

The discussions had brought out some unwelcome features of Jackson's character. He was not a diplomat. He had little inclination towards flexibility, and he took defeats personally. He clung stubbornly to his own opinions and found it difficult to see any good features in Continental legal practices. He had a short temper. He was pugnacious and his powerful drive towards some kind of ethereal legal upland where nation could talk to nation made negotiations over practicalities hard to complete.

Perhaps the idea that was to give the most trouble, right up until the last days of the trial, was the concept of conspiracy to commit crimes. Jackson had something of an obsession about this, while his colleagues would probably have been happy to limit the prosecution to crimes actually committed. Without Jackson's powerful advocacy, this charge would not have been considered separately at Nuremberg.

The four charges made at Nuremberg were each handled by the different national teams. Jackson and his American team were given the conspiracy charge, and this decision opened the way for some sordid politics. America considered itself to be the leading Allied nation and wanted to exert as much influence over the proceedings as possible. Jackson's attitude reflected this and in an internal memo he wrote that having the conspiracy charge would be 'the basis for keeping the bulk of the case in American hands'. He felt the primary function of the other national teams would be to gather evidence in their own spheres to support the conspiracy charge, and only incidentally pursue their own charges.

This attitude would have consequences during the trial itself.

On the 21st November 1945, all of Jackson's hard work and argument finally came to an end. He stood to address the International Military Tribunal with a speech opening the prosecution.

He had been working alone on this speech for many months. It had gone through many drafts, some of which survive, to reach a finely honed piece of rhetoric intended to sway the opinions of the judges, and of the outside world. The speech made a great impact inside the courtroom and beyond, and his words are still studied today.

To a European ear, the speech sounded florid and a little overblown, more of a Presidential address than a forensic analysis. Nonetheless, it was welcomed by his audience, professional colleagues and laymen alike. He emphasized the importance of the trial as being the first time great men were called to account for the criminal acts committed by the nation under their command. He rejected the idea that nations commit crime. 'Crimes are committed only by persons', he said, and they should accept the consequences of their actions.

Jackson spoke for most of the day. Everyone in court concentrated on his words, including the prisoners in the dock. When the speech ended, his colleagues crowded around to congratulate him, and the press coverage was uniformly good.

This speech of Jackson's was a high point for him, and for a while he stepped back to let other prosecutors handle the American case. His next appointment with the limelight lay far in the future – the cross-examination of Hermann Goering.

Sir David Maxwell-Fyfe KC

Sir David Patrick Maxwell-Fyfe was a practicing barrister and a respected Conservative politician.

Born in Edinburgh in 1900, his father was a school headmaster. Maxwell-Fyfe went on to study at Oxford, taking a break to serve with the Scots Guards in 1918-19. After graduation, he began his political career but studied law in his spare time. He was called to the bar in 1922.

Being a junior lawyer did not blunt his appetite for politics and he was given a chance to show his mettle by the Conservative party, fighting for an unwinnable seat in 1924. He continued to work for the Conservatives but was not favoured with a winnable seat until he won West Derby in 1935.

By this time, Maxwell-Fyfe's legal career had flourished. He was unusually hard-working and was rewarded with the status of King's Counsel in 1934 – the youngest KC in 250 years.

As Europe slid towards war, Maxwell-Fyfe was a main stream Conservative politician, supporting the Tory grandees who failed to stand up to Hitler and went down in history as failures. Once Czechoslovakia had been occupied by Germany, Maxwell-Fyfe joined the Territorial Army. When war broke out, he was taken into the Army's Judge Advocate-General's department.

In 1942, Churchill appointed Maxwell-Fyfe as Solicitor-General, and later Attorney-General. He was also knighted and made a Privy Councillor. He was now moving in the highest circles in the land.

As Solicitor-General, Maxwell-Fyfe became the leading member of the British prosecution team for Nuremberg. Unfortunately for him, Churchill and the Conservatives lost the post-war General Election in July 1945, and Maxwell-Fyfe was no longer Attorney-General. Sir Hartley Shawcross, from the new Labour government, took over leadership of the team. However, as the new government started on the massive project of rebuilding Britain, Hartley Shawcross could not be spared to attend the Tribunal in Nuremberg. The burden of the case remained with Maxwell-Fyfe, with Hartley Shawcross exercising oversight, and giving the opening and closing statements for the British team.

At Nuremberg, Maxwell-Fyfe was very much a team leader. His men were a small group of talented, practising barristers and he was able to handle them on a very light rein. His main management tool seems to have been 'Morning Prayers', a short meeting of the team every morning where progress was discussed and work allocated. Maxwell-Fyfe was able to draw the best out of everyone, and disagreements were rare.

The same was not true for the prosecution groups as a whole. As the trial progressed, prosecutors from the four nations had to work together and conflicts were inevitable. It usually fell to Maxwell-Fyfe to patch together compromises, smooth ruffled feathers and generally keep the prosecutors singing from the same song-sheet.

At the time of the Nuremberg trial, Maxwell-Fyfe was an experienced barrister, used to working on the courtroom floor. He had the reputation of being competent rather than brilliant but, most importantly, he was a meticulous worker. He prepared his courtroom appearances very carefully, marshalling his facts and documents together with lists of possible questions for witnesses. His aim was to control witness examinations by covering all possible answers to his planned line of questioning.

Maxwell-Fyfe did not have the reputation of a great cross-examiner, but his preparations always made him formidable. All his skills would be needed to confront Goering in the witness box.

The Cross Examination of Goering
18th March 1946 - Morning

Goering had begun giving his testimony on the 13th March and was questioned for three days by his lawyer, Dr Stahmer. This was followed by questions from counsel representing some of the other defendants. They were seeking details and clarifications that might assist the defence of their own clients.

Once these questions were over, the President of the Tribunal called on the Chief Prosecutors to begin their cross examinations, and Jackson took the floor.

The public mood at the time was ambivalent towards the Tribunal, but everyone wanted to hear what Goering had to say. The war had been over for almost a year, and the trial had been running for four months. In most of Europe, people were suffering from the effects of the war and this suffering was particularly acute for the people of Germany. Other countries, such as Poland or parts of the Soviet Union, had suffered grave loss and destruction, but they were busy building a new future. Germans were enduring the same sort of hardships, but could not get on with their future until they had understood and adapted to their past. Now the most senior surviving Nazi, the man who had been at Hitler's elbow through the 1930s and during the war, was about to face his prosecutors.

The Americans, in line with their desire to take the lead at the Tribunal, had taken charge of Goering's case. Jackson, as their chief prosecutor, had reached the highest point of his career as, before the world, he began the attempt to dismantle Goering's defences.

He began indirectly, apparently seeking to uncover Goering's opinions on the Nazi system and the reasons for adopting non-Democratic government in Germany. Goering answered confidently and described the way Hitler and the Nazis established their totalitarian state. Jackson permitted him to give detailed descriptions and explanations, and the bench even encouraged this at one point.

Reading the text of the cross examination set out coldly on the pages below, subjects that seem utterly abhorrent to most modern people (and most people at the time, if they had understood what had been done) were discussed and considered. Strangely, the discussions seem to treat horrifying criminal activity as normal, perhaps regrettable but necessary to the governance and prosperity of Germany. Concentration camps were normal, a product of the time. Political murders or the annexing of Austria were unfortunate but necessary. Jackson does not seem to portray any of these as crimes and, what is more, crimes that could be laid at least partly at the door of Goering.

For Goering, the most treacherous ground touched on in this first session was the Night of the Long Knives. Using the documents available, Jackson might have tied Goering closely to the planning of this operation, but he seemed content to accept Goering's position that the operation and subsequent executions were outside his influence.

As the court adjourned for lunch, Jackson had not damaged Goering's composure at all.

Testimony - Morning Session – 18th March 1946

Jackson You are perhaps aware that you are the only living man who can expound to us the true purposes of the Nazi Party and the inner workings of its leadership?

Goering I am perfectly aware of that.

Jackson You, from the very beginning, together with those who were associated with you, intended to overthrow and later did overthrow, the Weimar Republic?

Goering That was, as far as I am concerned, my firm intention.

Jackson And, upon coming to power, you immediately abolished parliamentary government in Germany?

Goering We found it to be no longer necessary. Also I should like to emphasize the fact that we were moreover the strongest parliamentary party, and had the majority. But you are correct, when you say that parliamentary procedure was done away with, because the various parties were disbanded and forbidden.

Jackson You established the Leadership Principle, which you have described as a system under which authority existed only at the top, and is passed downwards and is imposed on the people below; is that correct?

Goering In order to avoid any misunderstanding, I should like once more to explain the idea briefly, as I understand it. In German parliamentary procedure in the past responsibility rested with the highest officials, who were responsible for carrying out the anonymous wishes of the majorities, and it was they who exercised the authority. In the Leadership Principle we sought to reverse the direction, that is, the authority existed at the top and passed downwards, while the responsibility began at the bottom and passed upwards.

Jackson In other words, you did not believe in and did not permit government, as we call it, by consent of the governed, in which the people, through their representatives, were the source of power and authority?

Goering That is not entirely correct. We repeatedly called on the people to express unequivocally and clearly what they thought of our system, only it was in a different way from that previously adopted and from the system in practice in other countries. We chose the way of a so-called plebiscite. We also took the point of view that even a government founded on the Leadership Principle could maintain itself only if it was based in some way on the confidence of the people. If it no longer had such confidence, then it would have to rule with bayonets, and the Fuehrer was always of the opinion that that was impossible in the long run -- to rule against the will of the people.

Jackson But you did not permit the election of those who should act with authority by the people, but they were designated from the top downward continuously, were they not?

Goering Quite right. The people were merely to acknowledge the authority of the Fuehrer, or, let us say, to declare themselves in agreement with the Fuehrer. If they gave the Fuehrer their confidence, then it was their concern to exercise the other functions. Thus, not the individual persons were to be selected according to the will of the people, but solely the leadership itself.

Jackson Now, was this Leadership Principle supported and adopted by you in Germany because you believed that no people are capable of self-government, or because you believed that some may be, not the German people; or that no matter whether some of us are capable of using our own system, it should not be allowed in Germany?

Goering I beg your pardon, I did not quite understand the question, but I could perhaps answer it as follows:

I consider the Leadership Principle necessary because the system which previously existed, and which we called parliamentary or democratic, had brought Germany to the verge of ruin. I might perhaps in this connection remind you that your own President Roosevelt, as far as I can recall -- I do not want to quote it word for word -- declared, "Certain peoples in Europe have forsaken democracy, not because they did not wish for democracy as such, but because democracy had brought forth men who were too weak to give their people work and bread, and to satisfy them. For this reason the peoples have abandoned this system and the men belonging to it." There is much truth in that statement. This system had brought ruin by mismanagement and according to my own opinion, only an organization made up of a strong, clearly defined leadership hierarchy could restore order again. But, let it be understood, not against the will of the people, but only when the people, having in the course of time, and by means of a series of elections, grown stronger and stronger, had expressed their wish to entrust their destiny to the National Socialist leadership.

Jackson The principles of the authoritarian government which you set up required, as I understand you, that there be tolerated no opposition by political parties which might defeat or obstruct the policy of the Nazi Party?

Goering You have understood this quite correctly. By that time we had lived long enough with opposition and we had had enough of it. Through opposition we had been completely ruined. It was now time to have done with it and to start building up.

Jackson After you came to power, you regarded it necessary, in order to maintain power, to suppress all opposition parties?

Goering We found it necessary not to permit any more opposition, yes.

Jackson And you also held it necessary that you should suppress all individual opposition lest it should develop into a party of opposition?

Goering Insofar as opposition seriously hampered our work of building up, this opposition of individual persons was, of course, not tolerated. Insofar as it was simply a matter of harmless talk, it was considered to be of no consequence.

Jackson Now, in order to make sure that you suppressed the parties, and individuals also, you found it necessary to have a secret political police to detect opposition?

Goering I have already stated that I considered that necessary, just as previously the political police had existed, but on a firmer basis and larger scale.

Jackson And upon coming to power you also considered it

immediately necessary to establish concentration camps to take care of your incorrigible opponents?

Goering I have already stated that the reason for the concentration camps was not because it could be said, "Here are a number of people who are opposed to us and they must be taken into protective custody." Rather they were set up as a lightning measure against the functionaries of the Communist Party who were attacking us in the thousands, and who, since they were taken into protective custody, were not put in prison. But it was necessary, as I said, to erect a camp for them -- one, two, or three camps.

Jackson But you are explaining, as the high authority of this system, to men who do not understand it very well, and I want to know what was necessary to run the kind of system that you set up in Germany. The concentration camp was one of the things you found immediately necessary upon coming into power, was it not? And you set them up as a matter of necessity, as you saw it?

Goering That was faultily translated -- it went too fast. But I believe I have understood the sense of your remarks. You asked me if I considered it necessary to establish concentration camps immediately in order to eliminate opposition. Is that correct?

Jackson Your answer is "yes", I take it?

Goering Yes.

Jackson Was it also necessary, in operating this system, that you must not have persons entitled to public trials in independent courts? And you immediately issued an order that your political police would not be subject to court review or to court orders, did you not?

Goering You must differentiate between the two categories; those who had committed some act of treason against the new state, or those who might be proved to have committed such an act, were naturally turned over to the courts. The others, however, of whom one might expect such acts, but who had not yet committed them, were taken into protective custody, and these were the people who were taken to concentration camps. I am now speaking of what happened at the beginning. Later things changed a great deal. Likewise, if for political reasons -- to answer your question -- someone was taken into protective custody, that is, purely for reasons of state, this could not be reviewed or stopped by any court. Later, when some people were also taken into protective custody for non-political reasons, people who had opposed the system in some other way, I once, as Prussian

Prime Minister and Reich Minister of the Interior, I remember...

Jackson Let's omit that. I have not asked for that. If you will just answer my question, we shall save a great deal of time. Your counsel will be permitted to bring out any explanations you want to make.

You did prohibit all court review and considered it necessary to prohibit court review of the causes for taking people into what you called protective custody?

Goering That I answered very clearly, but I should like to make an explanation in connection with my answer.

Jackson Your counsel will see to that. Now, the concentration camps and the protective custody...

President Mr. Justice Jackson, the Tribunal thinks the witness ought to be allowed to make what explanation he thinks right in answer to this question.

Jackson The Tribunal thinks that you should be permitted to explain your answer now, and it will listen to your answers.

President I did not mean that to apply generally to his answers. I meant it to apply to this particular answer.

Goering In connection with your question that these cases could not be reviewed by the court, I want to say that a decree was issued through me and Frick jointly to the effect that those who were turned over to concentration camps were to be informed after 24 hours of the reason for their being turned over, and that after 48 hours, or some short period of time, they should have the right to an attorney. But this by no means rescinded my order that a review was not permitted by the courts of a politically necessary measure of protective custody. These people were simply to be given an opportunity of making a protest.

Jackson Protective custody meant that you were taking people into custody who had not committed any crimes but who, you thought, might possibly commit a crime?

Goering Yes. People were arrested and taken into protective custody who had not yet committed any crime, but who could be expected to do so if they remained free, just as extensive protective measures are being taken in Germany today on a tremendous scale.

Jackson Now, it is also a necessity, in the kind of state that you had, that you have some kind of organization to carry propaganda down to the people and to get their reaction and inform the leadership of it, is it not?

Goering The last part of that question has not been intelligibly translated.

Jackson Well, you had to have organizations to carry out orders and to carry your propaganda in that kind of state, didn't you?

Goering Of course, we carried on propaganda, and for this we had a propaganda organization.

Jackson And you carried that on through the Leadership Corps of the Nazi Party, did you not?

Goering The Leadership Corps was there, of course, partly to spread our ideas among the people. Secondly, its purpose was to lead and organize the people who made up the Party.

Jackson Through your system of Gauleiter and Kreisleiter down to Blockleiter, commands and information went down from the authority, and information as to the people's reactions came back to the leadership, didn't it?

Goering That is correct. The orders and commands that were to be given for propaganda or other purposes were passed down the grades as far as necessary. On the other hand, it was a matter of course that the reactions of the broad masses of the people were again transmitted upwards, through the various offices, in order to keep us informed of the mood of the people.

Jackson And you also had to have certain organizations to carry out orders -- executive organizations, organizations to fight for you if necessary, did you not?

Goering Yes, administrative organizations were, of course, necessary. I do not quite understand -- organizations to fight what?

Jackson Well, if you wanted certain people killed you had to have some organization that would kill them, didn't you? Rohm and the rest of them were not killed by Hitler's own hands nor by yours, were they?

Goering Rohm -- the Rohm affair I explained here clearly -- that was a matter of State necessity...

Jackson I did not ask you...

Goering ... and was carried out by the police.

Jackson But when it was State necessity to kill somebody, you had to have somebody to do it, didn't you?

Goering Yes, just as in other countries, whether it is called secret service or something else, I do not know.

Jackson And the SA, the SS, and the SD, organizations of that kind, were the organizations that carried out the orders and dealt with people on a physical level, were they not?

Goering The SA never received an order to kill anybody, neither did the SS, not in my time. Anyhow, I had no influence on it. I know that orders were given for executions, namely in the Rohm Putsch, and these were carried out by the police, that is, by a State organ.

Jackson What police?

Goering As far as I recall, through the Gestapo. At any rate, that was the organization that received the order. You see, it was a fight against enemies of the State.

Jackson And the SS was for the same purpose, was it not?

Goering Not in north Germany at that time; to what extent that was the case in south Germany, where the Gestapo and the SS were still separated, and who carried out the action in south Germany, I do not know.

Jackson Well, the SS carried out arrests and carried out the transportation of people to concentration camps, didn't they? You were arrested by the SS, weren't you?

Goering Yes, I say, yes; but later.

Jackson At what time did the SS perform this function of acting as the executor of the Nazi Party?

Goering After the seizure of power, when the police came to be more and more in the hands of Himmler. It is difficult for me to explain to an outsider where the SS or where the Gestapo was active. I have already said that the two of them worked very closely together. It is known that the SS guarded the camps and later carried out police functions.

Jackson And carried out other functions in the camps?

Goering To what functions do you refer?

Jackson They carried out all of the functions of the camps, didn't they?

Goering If an SS unit was guarding a camp and an SS leader happened to be the camp commander, then this unit carried out all the functions.

Jackson Now, this system was not a secret system. This entire system was openly avowed, its merits were publicly advocated by yourself and others, and every person entering into the Nazi Party was enabled to know the kind of system of government you were going to set up, wasn't he?

Goering Every person who entered the Party knew that we

embraced the Leadership Principle and knew the fundamental measures we wanted to carry out, so far as they were stated in the program. But not everyone who joined the Party knew down to the last detail what was going to happen later.

Jackson But this system was set up openly and was well known, was it not, in every one of its details? As to organization, everybody knew what the Gestapo was, did they not?

Goering Yes, everyone knew what the Gestapo was.

Jackson And what its program was in general, not in detail?

Goering I explained that program clearly. At the very beginning I described that publicly, and I also spoke publicly of the tasks of the Gestapo, and I even wrote about it for foreign countries.

Jackson And there was nothing secret about the establishment of a Gestapo as a political police, about the fact that people were taken into protective custody, about the fact that these were concentration camps? Nothing secret about those things, was there?

Goering There was at first nothing secret about it at all.

Jackson As a matter of fact, part of the effectiveness of a secret police and part of the effectiveness of concentration camp penalties is that the people do know that there are such agencies, isn't it?

Goering It is true that everyone knows that if he acts against the state he will end up in a concentration camp or will be accused of high treason before a court, according to the degree of his crime. But the original reason for creating the concentration camps was to keep there such people whom we rightfully considered enemies of the State.

Jackson Now, that is the type of government -- the government which we have just been describing -- the only type of government which you think is necessary to govern Germany?

Goering I should not like to say that the basic characteristic of this government and its most essential feature was the immediate setting up of the Gestapo and the concentration camps in order to, take care of our opponents, but that over and above that we had set down as our government program a great many far more important things, and that those other things were not the basic principles of our government.

Jackson But all of these things were necessary things, as I understood you, for purposes of protection?

Goering Yes, these things were necessary because of the opponents that existed.

Jackson And I assume that that is the only kind of government that you think can function in Germany under present conditions?

Goering Under the conditions existing at that time, it was, in my opinion, the only possible form, and it also demonstrated that Germany could be raised in a short time from the depths of misery, poverty, and unemployment to relative prosperity.

Jackson Now, all of this authority of the State was concentrated -- perhaps I am taking up another subject. Is it the intent to recess at this time?

President The Tribunal will adjourn.

[The Tribunal recessed until 1400 hours.]

The Cross Examination of Goering
18th March 1946 - Afternoon

Jackson started his afternoon questioning apparently searching for an admission that Goering was involved in planning aggressive war, and chose to look at Germany's attack on Soviet Russia.

In hindsight, it seems extremely unlikely that Goering was not involved in the planning of this invasion, and he must therefore have been guilty of conspiracy to wage aggressive war. This was one of the four main counts against the defendants, and the one closest to Jackson's heart. He needed to seize it like a terrier and keep worrying at the question until Goering's part in the conspiracy was pinned down.

Instead, Jackson drifted off into trying to establish exactly when Goering had admitted to himself that the war had been lost, his attitude to Hitler's final Will, and whether or not Goering had ordered the burning of the Reichstag, an accusation supported by nothing more than gossip.

He touched again on the Night of the Long Knives. Goering said he believed the official story, that Roehm and the SA were planning a coup d'état and had to be stopped (this might have been true but, if so, the planning was in a very early stage). We now know that somewhere between eighty and one hundred people were murdered over a period of two days. They included the top members of the SA and some political opponents who had no involvement but were a nuisance.

Again, Jackson did not seem to be interested in tying Goering directly to these crimes and moved on to ask about Goering's early days with the Nazi party and his feelings about Hitler.

Jackson asked Goering to comment on Hitler's attitude to the question of whether or not the USA would enter the war. This is a very interesting topic for historians, but added nothing to the cross examination.

Questioning turned to Goering's actions as head of the Four Year Plan, which had as its main task the preparation of Germany for war. Goering's efforts in the late 1930's certainly established the muscle that Germany needed to conquer Europe. Jackson needed to show that Goering's actions were part of a conspiracy to wage aggressive war, and not simply the prudent actions of any state preparing itself against the possibility of attack. Jackson did not ask the questions needed to prove this, and the rest of the prosecution lawyers must have reached the end of the day wondering what was happening to their case.

Testimony - Afternoon Session – 18th March 1946

Jackson Witness, you have related to us the manner in which you and others co-operated in concentrating all authority in the German State in the hands of the Fuehrer, is that right?

Goering I was speaking about myself and to what extent I had a part in it.

Jackson Is there any defendant in the box you know of who did not co-operate toward that end as far as was possible?

Goering That none of the defendants here opposed or obstructed the Fuehrer in the beginning is clear, but I should like to call your attention to the fact that we must always distinguish between different periods of time. Some of the questions that are being put to me are very general and, after all, we are concerned with a period extending over 24 to 25 years, if a comprehensive survey is to be made.

Jackson Now, I want to call your attention to the fruits of this system. You, as I understand it, were informed in 1940 of an impending attack by the German Army on Soviet Russia?

Goering I have explained just how far I was informed of these matters.

Jackson You believed an attack not only to be unnecessary, but also to be unwise from the point of view of Germany itself?

Goering At that particular time I was of the opinion that this attack should be postponed in order to carry through other tasks which I considered more important.

Jackson You did not see any military necessity for an attack at that time, even from the point of view of Germany?

Goering Naturally, I was fully aware of Russia's efforts in the deployment of her forces, but I hoped first to put into effect the other strategic measures, described by me, to improve Germany's position. I thought that the time required for these would ward off the critical moment. I well knew, of course, that this critical moment for Germany might come at any time after that.

Jackson I can only repeat my question, which I submit you have not answered.

Did you at that time see any military necessary for an attack by

Germany on Soviet Russia?

Goering I personally believed that at that time the danger had not yet reached its climax, and therefore the attack might not yet be necessary. But that was my personal view.

Jackson And you were the Number 2 man at that time in all Germany?

Goering It has nothing to do with my being second in importance. There were two conflicting points of view as regards strategy.

The Fuehrer, the Number 1 man, saw one danger, and I, as the Number 2 man, if you wish to express it so, wanted to carry out another strategic measure. If I had imposed my will every time, then I would probably have become the Number 1 man. But since the Number 1 man was of a different opinion, and I was only the Number 2 man, his opinion naturally prevailed.

Jackson I have understood from your testimony -- and I think you can answer this "yes" or "no," and I would greatly appreciate it if you would -- I have understood from your testimony that you were opposed, and told the Fuehrer that you were opposed, to an attack upon Russia at that time. Am I right or wrong?

Goering That is correct.

Jackson Now, you were opposed to it because you thought that it was a dangerous move for Germany to make; is that correct?

Goering Yes, I was of the opinion that the moment -- and I repeat this again -- had not come for this undertaking, and that measures should be taken which were more expedient as far as Germany was concerned.

Jackson And yet, because of the Fuehrer system, as I understand you, you could give no warning to the German people; you could bring no pressure of any kind to bear to prevent that step, and you could not even resign to protect your own place in history.

Goering These are several questions at once. I should like to answer the first one.

Jackson Separate them, if you wish.

Goering The first question was, I believe, whether I took the opportunity to tell the German people about this danger. I had no occasion to do this. We were at war, and such differences of opinion, as far as strategy was concerned, could not be brought before the public forum during war. I believe that never has happened in world history.

Secondly, as far as my resignation is concerned, I do not wish even to discuss that, for during the war I was an officer, a soldier, and I was not concerned with whether I shared an opinion or not. I had merely to serve my country as a soldier.

Thirdly, I was not the man to forsake someone, to whom I had given my oath of loyalty, every time he was not of my way of thinking. If that had been the case there would have been no need to bind myself to him from the beginning. It never occurred to me to leave the Fuehrer.

Jackson Insofar as you know, the German people were led into the war, attacking Soviet Russia under the belief that you favored it?

Goering The German people did not know about the declaration of war against Russia until after the war with Russia had started. The German people, therefore, had nothing to do with this. The German people were not asked; they were told of the fact and of the necessity for it.

Jackson At what time did you know that the war, as regards achieving the objectives that you had in mind, was a lost war?

Goering It is extremely difficult to say. At any rate, according to my conviction, relatively late -- I mean, it was only towards the end that I became convinced that the war was lost. Up till then I had always thought and hoped that it would come to a stalemate.

Jackson Well, in November 1941 the offensive in Russia broke down?

Goering That is not at all correct. We had reverses because of weather conditions, or rather, the goal which we had set was not reached. The push of 1942 proved well enough that there was no question of a military collapse. Some corps, which had pushed forward, were merely thrown back, and some were withdrawn. The totally unexpected early frost that set in was the cause of this.

Jackson You said, "relatively late." The expression that you used does not tell me anything, because I do not know what you regard as relatively late. Will you fix in terms, either of events or time, when it was that the conviction came to you that the war was lost?

Goering When, after 12 January 1945, the Russian offensive pushed forward to the Oder and at the same time the Ardennes offensive had not penetrated, it was then that I was forced to realize that defeat would probably set in slowly. Up to that time I had always hoped that, on the one side, the position at the Vistula toward the East and, on the other side, the position at the West Wall towards the West, could be held until the flow of the new mass produced weapons should bring about a slackening of the Anglo-American air war.

Jackson Now, will you fix that by date; you told us when it was by events.

Goering I just said January 1945; middle, or end of January 1945. After that there was no more hope.

Jackson Do you want it understood that, as a military man, you did not realize until January of 1945 that Germany could not be successful in the war?

Goering As I have already said, we must draw a sharp distinction between two possibilities: First, the successful conclusion of a war, and second, a war which ends by neither side being the victor. As regards a successful outcome, the moment when it was realized that that was no longer possible was much earlier, whereas the realization of the fact that defeat would set in did not come until the time I have just mentioned.

Jackson For some period before that, you knew that a successful termination of the war could only be accomplished if you could come to some kind of terms with the enemy; was that not true?

Goering Of course, a successful termination of a war can only be considered successful if I either conquer the enemy or, through negotiations with the enemy, come to a conclusion which guarantees me success. That is what I call a successful termination. I call it a draw, when I come to terms with the enemy. This does not bring me the success which victory would have brought but, on the other hand, it precludes a defeat. This is a conclusion without victors or vanquished.

Jackson But you knew that it was Hitler's policy never to negotiate and you knew that as long as he was the head of the Government the enemy would not negotiate with Germany, did you not?

Goering I knew that enemy propaganda emphasized that under no circumstances would there be negotiations with Hitler. That Hitler did not want to, negotiate under any circumstances, I also knew, but not in this connection. Hitler wanted to negotiate if there were some prospect of results; but he was absolutely opposed to hopeless and futile negotiations. Because of the declaration of the enemy in the West after the landing in Africa, as far as I remember, that under no circumstances would they negotiate with Germany but would force on her unconditional surrender, Germany's resistance was stiffened to the utmost and measures had to be taken accordingly. If I have no chance of concluding a war through negotiations, then it is useless to negotiate, and I must strain every nerve to bring about a change by a call to arms.

Jackson By the time of January 1945 you also knew that you were unable to defend the German cities against the air attacks of the Allies, did you not?

Goering Concerning the defence of German cities against Allied air attacks, I should like to describe the possibility of doing this as follows: Of itself ...

Jackson Can you answer my question? Time may not mean quite as much to you as it does to the rest of us. Can you not answer "yes" or "no"? Did you then know, at the same time that you knew that the war was lost, that the German cities could not successfully be defended against air attack by the enemy? Can you not tell us "yes" or "no"?

Goering I can say that I knew that, at that time, it was not possible.

Jackson And after that time it was well known to you that the air attacks which were continued against England could not turn the tide of war, and were designed solely to effect a prolongation of what you then knew was a hopeless conflict?

Goering I believe you are mistaken. After January 1945 there were no more attacks on England, except perhaps a few single planes, because at that time I needed all my petrol for the fighter planes for defence. If I had had bombers and oil at my disposal, then, of course, I should have continued such attacks up to the last minute as retaliation for the attacks which were being carried out on German cities, whatever our chances might have been.

Jackson What about robot attacks? Were there any robot attacks after January 1945?

Goering Thank God, we still had one weapon that we could use. I have just said that, as long as the fight was on, we had to hit back; and as a soldier I can only regret that we did not have enough of these V-1 and V-2 bombs, for an easing of the attacks on German cities could be brought about only if we could inflict equally heavy losses on the enemy.

Jackson And there was no way to prevent the war going on as long as Hitler was the head of the German Government, was there?

Goering As long as Hitler was the Fuehrer of the German people, he alone decided whether the war was to go on. As long as my enemy threatens me and demands absolutely unconditional surrender, I fight to my last breath, because there is nothing left for me except perhaps a chance that in some way fate may change, even though it seems hopeless.

Jackson Well, the people of Germany who thought it was time that the slaughter should stop had no means to stop it except revolution or assassination of Hitler, had they?

Goering A revolution always changes a situation, if it succeeds. That is a foregone conclusion. The murder of Hitler at this time, say January 1945, would have brought about my succession. If the enemy had given me the same answer, that is, unconditional surrender, and had held out those terrible conditions which had been intimated, I would have continued fighting whatever the circumstances.

Jackson There was an attack on Hitler's life on 20 July 1944?

Goering Unfortunately, yes.

Jackson And there came a time in 1945 when Hitler made a will in Berlin whereby he turned over the presidency of the Reich to your co-defendant, Admiral Doenitz. You know about that?

Goering That is correct. I read of this will here.

Jackson And in making his will and turning over the Government of Germany to Admiral Doenitz, I call your attention to this statement:

"Goering and Himmler, quite apart from their disloyalty to my person, have done immeasurable harm to the country and the whole nation by secret negotiations with the enemy which they conducted without my knowledge and against my wishes, and by illegally attempting to seize power in the State for themselves."

And by that will he expelled you and Himmler from the Party and from all offices of the State.

Goering I can only answer for myself. What Himmler did I do not know.

I neither betrayed the Fuehrer, nor did I at that time negotiate with a single foreign soldier. This will, or this final act of the Fuehrer's, is based on an extremely regrettable mistake, and one which grieves me deeply -- that the Fuehrer could believe in his last hours that I could ever be disloyal to him. It was all due to an error in the transmission of a radio report and perhaps to a misrepresentation which Bormann gave the Fuehrer. I myself never thought for a minute of taking over power illegally or of acting against the Fuehrer in any way.

Jackson In any event you were arrested and expected to be shot?

Goering That is correct.

Jackson Now, in tracing the rise of power of the Party you have omitted some such things as, for example, the Reichstag fire of 27 February 1933. There was a great purge following that fire, was there not, in which many people were arrested and many people were killed?

Goering I do not know of a single case where a man was killed because of the Reichstag fire, except that of the incendiary Van der Lubbe, who was sentenced by the court. The other two defendants in this trial were acquitted. Herr Thalmann was not, as you recently erroneously believed, accused; it was the communist representative, Torgler. He was acquitted, as was also the Bulgarian Dimitroff. Relatively few arrests were made in connection with the Reichstag fire. The arrests which you attribute to the Reichstag fire are the arrests of communist functionaries. These arrests, as I have repeatedly stated and wish to emphasize once more, had nothing to do with this fire. The fire merely precipitated their arrest and upset our carefully planned action, thus allowing several of the functionaries to escape.

Jackson In other words, you had lists of Communists already prepared at the time of the Reichstag fire of persons who should be arrested, did you not?

Goering We had always drawn up, beforehand, fairly complete lists of communist functionaries who were to be arrested. That had nothing to do with the fire in the German Reichstag.

Jackson They were immediately put into execution -- the arrests, I mean -- after the Reichstag fire?

Goering Contrary to my intention of postponing this action for a few days and letting it take place according to plan, thereby perfecting the arrangements, the Fuehrer ordered that same night that the arrests should follow immediately. This had the disadvantage, as I said, of precipitating matters.

Jackson You and the Fuehrer met at the fire, did you not?

Goering That is right.

Jackson And then and there you decided to arrest all the Communists that you had listed?

Goering I repeat again that the decision for their arrests had been reached some days before this; it simply meant that on that night they were immediately arrested. I would rather have waited a few days according to plan; then some of the important men would not have escaped.

Jackson   And the next morning the decree was presented to President Von Hindenburg, suspending the provisions of the constitution which we have discussed here, was it not?

Goering   I believe so, yes.

Jackson   Who was Karl Ernst?

Goering   Karl Ernst -- whether his first name was Karl I do not know -- was the SA leader of Berlin.

Jackson   And who was Helldorf?

Goering   Count Helldorf was the subsequent SA leader of Berlin.

Jackson   And Heines?

Goering   Heines was the SA leader of Silesia at that time.

Jackson   Now, it is known to you, is it not, that Ernst made a statement confessing that these three burned the Reichstag and that you and Goebbels planned and furnished the incendiary materials of liquid phosphorus and petroleum which were deposited by you in a subterranean passage for them to get, which passage led from your house to the Reichstag building? You knew of such a statement, did you not?

Goering   I do not know of any statement by the SA leader Ernst. But I do know of some fairytale published shortly after in the foreign press by Rohm's chauffeur. This was after 1934.

Jackson   But there was such a passage from the Reichstag building to your house, was there not?

Goering   On one side of the street is the Reichstag building, and opposite is the palace of the Reichstag president, The two are connected by a passage along which the wagons run which carry the coke for the central heating.

Jackson   And, in any event, shortly after this, Ernst was killed without a trial and without a chance to tell his story, was he not?

Goering   That is not correct. The Reichstag fire was in February 1933. Ernst was shot on 30 June 1934, because together with Rohm he had planned to overthrow the Government and had plotted against the Fuehrer. He, therefore, had a year and a quarter in which he could have made statements regarding the Reichstag fire, if he had wished to do so.

Jackson Well, he had begun to make statements, had he not, and you were generally being accused of burning the Reichstag building? You knew that, did you not? That was the ...

Goering That accusation that I had set fire to the Reichstag came from a certain foreign press. That could not bother me because it was not consistent with the facts. I had no reason or motive for setting fire to the Reichstag. From the artistic point of view I did not at all regret that the assembly chamber was burned; I hoped to build a better one. But I did regret very much that I was forced to find a new meeting place for the Reichstag and, not being able to find one, I had to give up my Kroll Opera House, that is, the second State Opera House, for that purpose. The opera seemed to me much more important than the Reichstag.

Jackson Have you ever boasted of burning the Reichstag building, even by way of joking?

Goering No. I made a joke, if that is the one you are referring to, when I said that, after this, I should be competing with Nero and that probably people would soon be saying that, dressed in a red toga and holding a lyre in my hand, I looked on at the fire and played while the Reichstag was burning. That was the joke. But the fact was that I almost perished in the flames, which would have been very unfortunate for the German people, but very fortunate for their enemies.

Jackson You never stated then that you burned the Reichstag?

Goering No. I know that Herr Rauschning said in the book which he wrote, and which has often been referred to here, that I had discussed this with him. I saw Herr Rauschning only twice in my life and only for a short time on each occasion. If I had set fire to the Reichstag, I would presumably have let that be known only to my closest circle of confidants, if at all. I would not have told it to a man whom I did not know and whose appearance I could not describe at all today. That is an absolute distortion of the truth.

Jackson Do you remember the luncheon on Hitler's birthday in 1942 at the Kasino, the officers' mess, at the headquarters of the Fuehrer in East Prussia?

Goering No.

Jackson You do not remember that? I will ask that you be shown the affidavit of General Franz Halder, and I call your attention to his statements which may refresh your recollection. I read it.

"On the occasion of a luncheon on the Fuehrer's birthday in 1942, the people around the Fuehrer turned the conversation to the Reichstag building and its artistic value. I heard with my own ears how Goering broke into the conversation and shouted: 'The only one who really knows the Reichstag is I, for I set fire to it.' And saying this he slapped his thigh."

Goering This conversation did not take place and I request that I be confronted with Herr Halder. First of all, I want to emphasize that what is written here is utter nonsense. It says, "The only one who really knows the Reichstag is I." The Reichstag was known to every representative in the Reichstag. The fire took place only in the general assembly room, and many hundreds or thousands of people knew this room as well as I did. A statement of this type is utter nonsense. How Herr Halder came to make that statement I do not know. Apparently that bad memory, which also let him down in military matters, is the only explanation.

Jackson You know who Halder is?

Goering Only too well.

Jackson Can you tell us what position he held in the German Army?

Goering He was Chief of the General Staff of the Army, and I repeatedly pointed out to the Fuehrer, after the war started, that he would at least have to find a chief who knew something about such matters.

Jackson Now, the Rohm purge you have left a little indefinite. What was it that Rohm did that he was shot? What acts did he commit?

Goering Rohm planned to overthrow the Government, and it was intended to kill the Fuehrer also.. He wanted to follow it up by a revolution, directed in the first place against the Army, the officers' corps -- those groups which he considered to be reactionary.

Jackson And you had evidence of that fact?

Goering We had sufficient evidence of that fact.

Jackson But he was never tried in any court where he would have a chance to tell his story as you are telling yours, was he?

Goering That is correct. He wanted to bring about a Putsch and therefore the Fuehrer considered it right that this thing should be nipped in the bud -- not by a court procedure, but by smashing the revolt immediately.

Jackson Were the names of the people who were killed in that purge, following the arrest of Rohm, ever published?

Goering Some of the names, yes; but not all of them, I believe.

Jackson Who actually killed Rohm? Do you know?

Goering I do not know who personally carried out this action.

Jackson To what organization was the order given?

Goering That I do not know either, because the shooting of Rohm was decreed by the Fuehrer and not by me, for I was competent in north Germany.

Jackson And who took into custody those who were destined for concentration camps, and how many were there?

Goering The police carried out the arrest of those who were, first of all, to be interrogated, those who were not so seriously incriminated and of whom it was not known whether they were incriminated or not. A number of these people were released very soon, others not until somewhat later. Just how many were arrested in this connection I cannot tell you. The arrests were made by the police.

Jackson The Gestapo, you mean?

Goering I assume so.

Jackson And if Milch testified that he saw 700 or 800 in Dachau in 1935, there must have been a very much larger number arrested, since you say many were released. Do you know the number that were arrested?

Goering I state again, I do not know exactly how many were arrested because the necessary arrests, or the arrest of those who were considered as having a part in this, did not go through me. My action ended, so to speak, on the date when the revolt was smashed. I understood Milch a little differently and I sent a note to my counsel in order that it be made clear, through a question whether Milch meant by these 700 people those concerned with the Rohm Putsch or whether he meant to say that he saw altogether 700 arrested persons there. That is the way I understood it. But to clarify this statement we should have to question Milch again, for I believe this number of 500, 600, or 700, to be far too high for the total number of people arrested in connection with the Rohm Putsch.

Jackson Among those who were killed were Von Schleicher and his wife. He was one of your political opponents, was he not?

Goering That is right.

Jackson And also Erich Klausner, who had been Chief of the Catholic Action of Germany?

Goering Klausner was likewise among those who were shot. Actually, it was Klausner's case which caused me, as I stated recently, to ask the Fuehrer to give immediate orders to cease any further action, since, in my opinion, Klausner was quite wrongfully shot.

Jackson And Strasser, who had been the former Number 2 man to Hitler and had disagreed with him in December 1932 -- Strasser was killed, was he not?

Goering Of Strasser it cannot be said that he was Number 2 man after Hitler. He played an extremely important role within the Party before the seizure of power, but he was banned from the Party already before the seizure of power. Strasser participated in this revolt and he was also shot.

Jackson And when it got down to a point where there were only two left on the list yet to be killed, you intervened and asked to have it stopped; is that correct?

Goering No, that is not entirely correct. I made it fairly clear and should like to repeat briefly that not when there were only two left on the list did I intervene; I intervened when I saw that many were shot who were not concerned with this matter. And when I did so, two persons were left who had taken a very active part, and the Fuehrer himself had ordered that they be shot. The Fuehrer was particularly furious with one of them, the chief instigator of the action. What I wanted to make clear was that I said to the Fuehrer, "It is better for you to give up the idea of having these two main perpetrators executed, and put an end to the whole thing immediately." That is what I meant.

Jackson What date was that? Did you fix the time?

Goering Yes, I can give you a definite time. As far as I recall, the decisive day was Saturday; on Saturday evening between 6 and 7 o'clock the Fuehrer arrived by plane from Munich. My request to stop the action was made on Sunday, some time between 2 and 3 o'clock in the afternoon.

Jackson And what happened to the two men who were left on the list -- were they ever brought to trial?

Goering No. One, as far as I remember, was taken to a concentration camp, and the other was for the time being placed under a sort of house arrest, if I remember correctly.

Jackson Now, going back to the time when you met Hitler; you said that he was a man who had a serious and definite aim, that he was not content with the defeat of Germany and with the Versailles Treaty; do you recall that?

Goering I am very sorry, the translation was rather defective and I cannot understand it. Please repeat.

Jackson When you met Hitler, as I understand your testimony, you found a man with a serious and definite aim, as you said, in that he was not content with the defeat of Germany in the previous war and was not content with the Versailles Treaty.

Goering I think you did not quite understand me correctly here, for I did not put it that way at all. I stated that it had struck me that Hitler had very definite views of the impotency of protest; secondly, that he was of the opinion that Germany must be freed from the dictate of Versailles. It was not only Adolf Hitler; every German, every patriotic German had the same feelings; and I, being an ardent patriot, bitterly felt the shame of the dictate of Versailles, and I allied myself with the man about whom I felt that he perceived most clearly the consequences of this dictate, and that probably he was the man who would find the ways and means to set it aside. All the other talk in the Party about Versailles was, pardon the expression, mere twaddle.

Jackson So, as I understand you, from the very beginning, publicly and notoriously, it was the position of the Nazi Party that the Versailles Treaty must be set aside and that protest was impotent for that purpose?

Goering From the beginning it was the aim of Adolf Hitler and his movement to free Germany from the oppressive fetters of Versailles, that is, not from the whole Treaty of Versailles, but from those terms which were strangling Germany's future.

Jackson And to do it by war, if necessary?

Goering We did not debate about that at all at the time. We debated only about the foremost condition, that Germany should acquire a different political structure, which alone would enable her to raise objections to this dictate, this one-sided dictate -- everybody always called it a peace, whereas we Germans always called it a dictate -- and not merely objections, but such objections as would demand consideration.

Jackson That was the means -- the means was the reorganization of the German State, but your aim was to get rid of what you call the dictate of Versailles.

Goering Liberation from these terms of the dictate of Versailles, which in the long run would make German life impossible, was the aim and the intention. But by that we did not go as far as to say, "We want to wage war on our enemies and be victorious." Rather, the aim was to suit the methods to the political events. Those were the basic considerations.

Jackson And it was for that end that you and all of the other persons who became members of the Nazi Party gave to Hitler all power to make decisions for them, and agreed, in their oath of office, to give him obedience?

Goering Again here are several questions. Question One: The fight against the dictate of Versailles was for me the most decisive factor in joining the Party. For others, perhaps, other points of the program or of the ideology, which seemed more important, may have been more decisive. Giving the Fuehrer absolute powers was not a basic condition for getting rid of Versailles, but for putting into practice our conception of the Leadership Principle. To give him our oath before he became the head of the State was, under the conditions then existing, a matter of course for those who considered themselves members of his select leadership corps. I do not know and I cannot tell exactly, just how the oath was given before the seizure of power; I can only tell you what I myself did. After a certain period of time, when I had acquired more insight into the Fuehrer's personality, I gave him my hand and said: "I unite my fate with yours for better or for worse: I dedicate myself to you in good times and in bad, even unto death." I really meant it -- and still do.

Jackson If you would answer three or four questions for me "yes" or "no," then I would be quite willing to let you give your entire version of this thing. In the first place, you wanted a strong German State to overcome the conditions of Versailles.

Goering We wanted a strong State anyhow, regardless of Versailles; but in order to get rid of Versailles the State had, first of all, to be strong, for a weak State never makes itself heard; that we know from experience.

Jackson And the Fuehrer principle you adopted because you thought it would serve the ends of a strong State?

Goering Correct.

Jackson And this aim, which was one of the aims of the Nazi Party, to modify the conditions of Versailles, was a public and notorious aim in which the people generally joined -- it was one of your best means of getting people to join with you, was it not?

Goering The dictate of Versailles was such that every German, in my opinion, could not help being in favor of its modification, and there is no doubt that this was a very strong inducement for joining the movement.

Jackson Now, a number of the men who took part in this movement are not here; and, for the record, there is no doubt in your mind, is there, that Adolf Hitler is dead?

Goering I believe there can be no doubt about that.

Jackson And the same is true of Goebbels?

Goering Goebbels, I have no doubt about that, for I heard from someone whom I trust completely, that he saw Goebbels dead.

Jackson And you have no doubt of the death of Himmler, have you?

Goering I am not certain of that, but I think that you must be certain, since you know much more about it than I, as he died a prisoner of yours. I was not there.

Jackson You have no doubt of the death of Heydrich, have you?

Goering I am absolutely certain about that.

Jackson And probably of Bormann?

Goering I am not absolutely certain of this. I have no proof. I do not know, but I assume so.

Jackson And those are the chief persons in your testimony, who have been mentioned as being responsible -- Hitler for everything, Goebbels for inciting riots against the Jews, Himmler, who deceived Hitler, and Bormann, who misled him about his will?

Goering The influence exerted on the Fuehrer varied at different times. The chief influence on the Fuehrer, at least up till the end of 1941 or the beginning of 1942, if one can speak of influence at all, was exerted by me. From then until 1943 my influence gradually decreased, after which it rapidly dwindled. All in all, I do not believe anyone had anything like the influence on the Fuehrer that I had. Next to me, or apart from me, if one can speak of influence at all, Goebbels, with whom the Fuehrer was together quite a good deal, exerted an influence in a certain direction from the very beginning. This influence wavered for a time and was very slight, and then increased greatly in the last years of the war, for it was easy to win influence by means of ...

Before the seizure of power and during the years immediately following the seizure of power, Hess had a certain influence, but only in regard to his special sphere. Then, in the course of the years, Himmler's influence increased. From the end of 1944 on this influence decreased rapidly. The most decisive influence on the Fuehrer during the war, and especially from about 1942 -- after Hess went out in 1941 and a year had elapsed -- was exerted by Herr Bormann. The latter had, at the end, a disastrously strong influence. That was possible only because the Fuehrer was filled with profound mistrust after 20 July, and because Bormann was with him constantly and reported on and described to him all matters. Broadly speaking, these are the persons who had influence at one time or another.

Jackson You took over a special intelligence organization in 1933 which was devoted to monitoring the telephone conversations of public officials and others inside and outside of Germany, did you not?

Goering I have explained that I had erected a technical apparatus which, as you said, monitored the conversations of important foreigners to and from foreign countries -- telegrams and wireless communications which were transmitted not only from Germany to foreign countries, but also from one foreign country to the other through the ether, and which were intercepted. It also monitored telephone conversations within Germany of: (1) all important foreigners; (2) important firms, at times; and (3) persons who for any reason of a political or police nature were to be watched.

In order to prevent any abuse on the part of the police, this department had to obtain my personal permission when it was to listen to telephone conversations. Despite this there could, of course, be uncontrolled tapping of wires at the same time, just as that is technically possible everywhere today.

Jackson You kept the results of those reports to yourself, did you not?

Goering No; this was the procedure: These reports in which the Foreign Office was interested were released to the Foreign Office. Those reports which were important to the Fuehrer went to the Fuehrer. Those which were important to the military authorities went to the Minister of War, or to the Air Ministry, or to the Ministry of Economy. I or my deputy decided whether a report was important for this or that office. There was a man there whose job and responsibility it was to see that these secret reports were submitted only to the chief. I could, of course, order at any time that this or that report should be exclusively for my knowledge and not be handed on. That was always possible.

Jackson You had a good deal of difficulty with other police authorities who wanted to get possession of that organization, did you not?

Goering That is correct. The police did strive to get this instrument into their hands. But they did not get it from me, and perhaps they kept a watch of their own here and there. But the decisive control which had to be directed through the Ministry of Posts could technically be ordered only by me.

Jackson You have listened to the evidence of the prosecution against all of the defendants of this case, have you not?

Goering Yes.

Jackson Is there any act of any of your co-defendants which you claim was not one reasonably necessary to carry out the plans of the Nazi Party?

Goering At present those are only assertions by the prosecution; they are not yet facts which have been proved. In these assertions there are a number of actions which would not have been necessary.

Jackson Will you specify which acts, of which defendants, you claim, are beyond the scope of the plans of the Party?

Goering That is a very difficult question which I cannot answer straight away and without the data.

Stahmer I object to this question. I do not believe that this is a question of fact, but rather of judgment, and that it is not possible to give an answer to such a general question.

President Mr. Justice Jackson, the Tribunal thinks that the question is somewhat too wide.

Jackson You have said that the program of the Nazi Party was to rectify certain injustices which you considered in the Treaty of Versailles; and I ask you whether it is not a fact that your program went considerably beyond any matter dealt with in that Treaty?

Goering Of course, the program contained a number of other points which had nothing to do with the Treaty of Versailles.

Jackson I call your attention to a statement in *Mein Kampf* as follows:

"The boundaries of 1914 do not mean anything for the future of the German nation. They did not constitute a defence in the past nor do they constitute a power in the future. They will not give to the German people inner security or ensure their food supply, nor do these boundaries appear to be favorable or satisfactory from a military point of view."

That is all true, is it not?

Goering I should like to reread the original passage in *Mein Kampf* in order to determine if it is exactly as you have read it. I assume that it is correct. If so, I can reply that this is the text of a public book and not the Party program.

Jackson The first country to be absorbed by Germany was Austria, and it was not a part of Germany before the first World War, and had not been taken from Germany by the Treaty of Versailles; is that correct?

Goering For this very reason this point was distinctly separated from Versailles in the program. Austria is directly connected with Versailles only insofar as the right of self-determination, as proclaimed there, was most gravely infringed; for Austria and the purely German population were not allowed the Anschluss which they wanted to see accomplished as early as 1918, after the revolution.

Jackson The second territory taken by Germany was Bohemia, then Moravia, and then Slovakia. These were not taken from Germany by the Treaty of Versailles, nor were they part of Germany before the first World War.

Goering As far as the Sudetenland is concerned the same applies as for Austria. The German representatives of the German Sudetenland likewise sat in the Austrian Parliament, and under their leader, Lottmann, cast the same vote. It is different in the case of the last act, that is, the declaration of the Protectorate. These parts of Czech territory, especially Bohemia and Moravia, were not constituent parts of the smaller German Reich before the Treaty of Versailles, but formerly they had been united to the German Reich for centuries. That is an historical fact.

Jackson You still have not answered my question, although you answered everything else. They were not taken from you by the Treaty of Versailles, were they?

Goering Of course Austria was taken away by the Versailles Treaty and likewise the Sudetenland, for both territories, had it not been for the Treaty of Versailles and the Treaty of St. Germain, would have become German territories through the right of the people to self-determination. To this extent they have to do with it.

Jackson You have testified, have you not, on interrogation, that it was Hitler's information that the United States would never go to war, even if attacked, and that he counted on the isolationists of that country to keep it out of war?

Goering This interrogation must have been recorded entirely incorrectly. That is the very reason why I refused from the beginning to give my oath to these interrogations before I had been able to look carefully at the German transcript and determine whether it had been correctly understood and translated. Only once, and that was on the part of the Russian Delegation, was a completely correct transcript submitted to me. I signed it page by page and thereby acknowledged it. Now, as far as this statement is concerned, I should like to put it right. I said that, at first, the Fuehrer did not believe that America would intervene in the war, and that he was confirmed in this belief by the attitude of the isolationist press, while I, on the contrary, unfortunately feared from the very beginning that America would in any case intervene in the war. Such nonsense -- I hope you will excuse me -- as to say that America would not come into the war even if she were attacked, you will understand that I could never have uttered, because, if a country is attacked, it defends itself.

Jackson Do you know Axel Wennergren?

Goering He is a Swede whom I have seen two or three times.

Jackson You talked with him about this subject, did you not?

Goering About the subject of America's entering the war I can very well have talked with him; it is even probable,

Jackson You told him that a democracy could not mobilize and would not fight, did you not?

Goering I did not tell him any such nonsense, for we had one democracy as our chief enemy, namely England, and how this democracy would fight we knew from the last World War, and we experienced it again during this war. When I talked with Wennergren, the war with England was in full swing.

Jackson You have testified on interrogation, if I understand you correctly, that there were at all times two basic ideas in Hitler's mind, either to ally himself with Russia and seek increase in living space through the acquisition of colonies, or to ally himself with Britain and seek acquisition of territories in the East. But in view of his orientation, he would very much have preferred to ally himself with Great Britain, is that true?

Goering That is correct. I need only to refer to the book *Mein Kampf*, where these things were set down in thorough detail by Hitler.

Jackson Now, as early as 1933 you began a real program to rearm Germany regardless of any treaty limitations, did you not?

Goering That is not correct.

Jackson All right; tell us when you started.

Goering After all the proposals of disarmament which the Fuehrer made were refused, that is, shortly after our withdrawal from the disarmament conference he made several proposals for a limitation; but, since these were not taken seriously or discussed, he ordered a complete rearmament. At the end of 1933 already certain slight preparations were started by me personally, to the extent that I had made some inconsiderable preparations in regard to the air and had also undertaken a certain militarization of the uniformed police. But that was done by me personally; I bear the responsibility.

Jackson Well, then, the militarization of the police auxiliary was not a state affair. It was your personal affair. What do you mean by that?

Goering Not the auxiliary police, but the municipal police; that is, there was one uniformed police force which had simply police duty on the streets, and a second which was grouped in formations and was at our disposal for larger operations -- not created by us, let it be understood; but existing at the time of the seizure of power. This municipal police, which was grouped in units, uniformed, armed, and housed in barracks, I formed very soon into a strong military instrument by taking these men out of the police service and having them trained more along military lines and giving them machine guns and such things, in addition to their small arms. This I did on my own responsibility. These formations were taken into the Armed Forces as regular Army units when the Armed Forces Law was declared.

Jackson I want to ask you some questions from your interrogation of the 17th day of October, 1945. 1 will first read you the questions and answers as they appear in the interrogations and I shall then ask you whether you gave those answers, and then you can make the explanations if you desire, and I assume you do. The interrogation reads:

"I wanted to ask you today about some of the economic history of the period. When was the armament program first discussed, that is, the rearmament program? What year?"

Answer: "Immediately; in 1933."

Question: "In other words, Schacht had assumed the obligation at that time already, to raise funds for the rearmament program?"

Answer: "Yes. But, of course, in co-operation with the Minister of Finance."

Question: "During the years 1933 to 1935, before general conscription came in, naturally, the rearmament was a secret rearmament, was it not?"

Answer: "Yes."

Question: "So that money that was used outside of the budget would have to be raised by some secret means not to be known to foreign nations?"

Answer: "Yes, unless they could be raised from normal Army funds."

Question: "That is to say, you had a small budget for the standing 100,000 man Army which was open, and the rest of the rearmament had to be from secret sources?"

"Answer: Yes."

Were you asked those questions and did you give these answers, in substance?

Goering More or less; generally speaking that is correct. I have these remarks to make: Firstly, I was asked when rearmament had been discussed, not when it had been started. It had, of course, been discussed already in the year 1933, because it was clear at once that our government had to do something about it, that is to say, to demand that the others should disarm, and, if they did not disarm, that we should rearm. These things required discussion. The conclusion of the discussion and the formulation into a definite order followed after the failure of our attempts to get other countries to disarm. As soon as we, or rather the Fuehrer, saw that his proposals would not be accepted under any circumstances, a gradual rearmament, of course, began to take place. There was no reason whatsoever why we should inform the world about what we were doing in the way of rearmament. We were under no obligation to do that, nor was it expedient.

Herr Schacht, in the year 1933 at the very beginning, could not raise any funds because at the start he held no office. He was able to do this only at a later date. And here it was understandable that the funds had to be raised through the Minister of Finance and the President of the Reichsbank according to the wishes and the orders of the Fuehrer, especially as we had left no doubt that, if the other side did not disarm, we would rearm. That had already been set down on our Party program since 1921, and quite openly.

Jackson Is it not a fact that on the 21st of May 1935, by a secret decree, Schacht was named Plenipotentiary for the War Economy?

Goering The date -- if you will kindly submit the decree to me, then I can tell you exactly. I have not the dates of decrees and laws in my head, especially if they do not have anything to do with me personally; but that can be seen from the decree.

Jackson At any event, shortly after he was named, he suggested you as Commissioner for Raw Materials and Foreign Currency, did he not?

Goering If Herr Schacht made this suggestion shortly after his appointment, then that appointment could not have taken place until 1936, because not until the summer of 1936 did Herr Schacht, together with the Minister of War, Von Blomberg, make the proposal that I should become Commissioner for Raw Materials and Foreign Currency.

Jackson Well, I ask you if you did not give this answer to the American interrogator on the 10th day of October 1945, referring to Schacht:

"He made the suggestion that I was to become the Commissioner for Raw Materials and Foreign Currency. He had the idea that, in that position, I could give the Minister for Economics and the President of the Reichsbank valuable support."

How did you give that answer, and is that information correct?

Goering Will you please repeat.

Jackson Referring to Schacht, the record shows that you said:

"He made the suggestion that I was to become the Commissioner for Raw Materials and Foreign Currency. He had the idea that, in that position, I could give the Minister for Economics and the President of the Reichsbank valuable support."

Goering That is absolutely correct, with the exception of the word "Reichstagsprasident;" that ought to be President of the Reichsbank.

Jackson Yes. That is the way I have it.

Goering It sounded like "Reichstagsprasident" over the earphones.

Jackson "Moreover, he was very outspoken in the suggestion that he and Blomberg made, that I should be put in charge of the Four Year Plan. However, Schacht's idea was that I did not know very much about economy, and that he could easily hide behind my back."

Goering That I said the other day quite clearly.

Jackson Now, from that time on you and Schacht collaborated for some time in preparing a rearmament program, did you not?

Goering From that time on I worked together with Schacht in economic matters and covered the whole field of German economy, including the armament program, which of course was a *sine qua non* for the reassumed German military sovereignty.

Jackson And you and he had some jurisdictional differences and executed an agreement settling your different spheres of authority, did you not?

Goering Yes.

Jackson And that was in 1937 on the 7th of July, right?

Goering On that day a certain proposal for a settlement was made, but this did not lead to anything final being accomplished. That was because of the nature of the two posts and our personalities. Both of us, I, as Delegate for the Four Year Plan, and Herr Schacht, as Minister of Economics and President of the Reichsbank, were able to exercise very great influence on German economy. As Herr Schacht also had a very, strong personality and felt his position keenly, and I likewise was not inclined to hide my light under a bushel, whether we were friends or not we could not help getting in each other's way because of this question of authority, and one of us had finally to give in to the other.

Jackson And there came a time when he left the Ministry and the Reichsbank?

Goering First he resigned from the Reich Ministry of Economy in November 1937, and, as far as I know, he resigned as President of the Reichsbank at the end of 1938, but I cannot be certain about that date.

Jackson There was no disagreement between you and him that the program of rearmament should be carried through, was there? You disagreed only in the methods of doing it.

Goering I assume that Herr Schacht also, as a good German, was, of course, ready to put all his strength at the disposal of Germany's rearmament, in order that Germany should be strong; and therefore differences could have occurred only in regard to methods, for neither Herr Schacht nor I was arming for a war of aggression.

Jackson And after he left the rearmament work he remained as a Minister without Portfolio and sat in the Reichstag for some time, did he?

Goering That is correct. The Fuehrer wished it because, I believe, he wanted in this way to express his recognition of Herr Schacht.

Jackson And do you recall the time when you considered the calling up of 15-year-olds, the conscription of 15-year-olds?

Goering During the war you mean?

Jackson Yes.

Goering It was a question of Air Force auxiliaries, that is correct. They were 15- or 16-year-olds, I do not remember exactly which, and were called in as Air Force auxiliaries.

Jackson I will ask that you be shown Document Number 3700-PS and ask you whether you received from Schacht the letter of which that is a carbon copy.

[The document was handed to the witness.]

Goering Yes, I certainly did receive that letter. The year is not given here; that is missing in the copy.

Jackson Could you fix, approximately, the date of its receipt?

Goering It says here 3rd of November, but from the incidents described on the other side, I assume it must be 1943. On this copy the year, strangely enough, is not given, but I believe it was in the year 1943, 1 received this letter.

Jackson Did you reply to Document 3700-PS? Did you reply to this letter?

Goering I cannot say that today with certainty -- possibly.

Jackson Now, the Four Year Plan had as its purpose to put the entire economy in a state of readiness for war, had it not?

Goering I have explained that it had two tasks to fulfill -- 1) to safeguard German economy against crises, that is to say, to make it immune from export fluctuations, and, as regards food, from harvest fluctuations, as far as possible; and 2) to make it capable of withstanding a blockade, that is to say, in the light of experiences in the first World War, to put it on such a basis that in a second World War a blockade would not have such disastrous consequences. That the Four Year Plan in this respect was a basic prerequisite for the entire building-up and expansion of the armament industry goes without saying. Without it the rearmament industry could not have been shaped in this way.

Jackson To get a specific answer, if possible, did you not say in a letter to Schacht, dated the 18th day of December 1936, that you saw it to be your task, using these words, "within 4 years to put the entire economy in a state of readiness for war"? Did you say that or did you not?

Goering Of course I said that.

Jackson Now, do you recall the report of Blomberg in 1937 in which -- and you may examine if you wish Document Number C-175 -- in which he starts his report by saying:

"The general political position justifies the supposition that Germany need not expect an attack from any side."

Goering That may have been quite possible at that moment. I took a most reassuring view of the German situation in 1937. It was after the Olympic games and at that time the general situation was extraordinarily calm. But that had nothing to do with the fact that I felt obliged, quite apart from passing fluctuations from a calmer to a more tense atmosphere, to make German economy ready for war and proof against crises or blockades, for exactly 1 year later incidents of a different nature occurred.

Jackson Well now, does not Blomberg continue:

"Grounds for this are, in addition to the lack of desire for war in almost all nations, particularly the Western Powers, the deficiencies in the preparedness for war of a number of states, and of Russia in particular"?

That was the situation in 1937, was it not?

Goering That is the way Herr Von Blomberg saw the situation. Concerning the readiness for war in Russia, Herr Von Blomberg, in the same way as all those representatives of our Reichswehr mentality, was always really mistaken in contrast to the opinion expressed in other quarters with regard to Russian armaments. This is merely the opinion of Herr Von Blomberg -- not the Fuehrer's, not mine, and not the opinion of other leading people.

Jackson That, however, was the report of the Commander-in-Chief of the Armed Forces on the 24th of June 1937, was it not?

Goering That is correct.

Jackson You organized, 1 month later, the Hermann Goering Works?

Goering Right.

Jackson And the Hermann Goering Works were concerned with putting Germany in the condition of readiness for war, were they not?

Goering No, that is not right. The Hermann Goering Works were at first concerned solely with the mining of German iron ore in the region of Salzgitter and in a district in the Oberpfalz, and, after the annexation, with the iron ore works in Austria. The Hermann Goering Works first established exclusively mining and refining plants for this ore and foundries. Only much later steel works and rolling mills were added, that is to say, an industry.

Jackson The Hermann Goering Works were a part of the Four Year Plan, were they not?

Goering That is right.

Jackson And you have already said that the Four Year Plan had as its purpose to put the economy in a state of readiness for war; and the Hermann Goering Works were organized to exploit ore mining and iron smelting resources and to carry the process through to completed guns and tanks, were they not?

Goering No, that is not correct; the Hermann Goering Works had at first no armament works of their own, but merely produced, as I again repeat, the basic product, steel, crude steel.

Jackson Well, at all events, you continued your efforts and on the 8th of November 1943, you made a speech describing those efforts to the Gauleiter in the Fuehrer building at Munich, is that right?

Goering I do not know the exact date, but about that time I made a short speech, one of a series of speeches, to the Gauleiter about the air situation, as far as I remember, and also perhaps about the armament situation. I do not remember the words of that speech, since I was never asked about it until now; but the facts are correct.

Jackson Well, let me remind you if you used these terms, refreshing your recollection:

"Germany, at the beginning of the war, was the only country in the world possessing an operative, fighting air force. The other countries had split their air fleets up into army and navy air fleets and considered the air arm primarily as a necessary and important auxiliary of the other branches of the forces. In consequence, they lacked the instrument which is alone capable of dealing concentrated and effective blows, namely, an operative air force. In Germany we had gone ahead on those lines from the very outset, and the main body of the Air Force was disposed in such a way that it could thrust deeply into the hostile areas with strategic effect, while a lesser portion of the air force, consisting of Stukas and, of course, fighter planes, went into action on the front line in the battlefields. You all know what wonderful results were achieved by these tactics and what superiority we attained at the very beginning of the war through this modern kind of air force."

Goering That is entirely correct; I certainly did say that, and what is more, I acted accordingly. But in order that this be understood and interpreted correctly, I must explain briefly:

In these statements I dealt with two separate opinions on air strategy, which are still being debated today and without a decision having been reached. That is to say: Should the air force form an auxiliary arm of the army and the navy and be split up, to form a constituent part of the army and the navy, or should it be a separate branch of the armed forces? I explained that for nations with a very large navy it is perhaps understandable that such a division should be made. From the very beginning, thank God, we made the correct, consistent decision to build up a strong -- I emphasize the word "strong" -- and independent Air Force along with the Army and the Navy; and I described how we passed from a tentative air force to an operative air force.

As an expert I am today still of the opinion that only an operative air force can have a decisive effect. I have also explained, in regard to two- and four-engine bombers, that at first I was quite satisfied with the two-engine bombers because, firstly, I did not have four-engine bombers; and secondly, the operational radius of the two-engine bombers was wide enough for the enemy with whom we had to deal at that time. I further pointed out that the main reason for the swift ending of the campaign in Poland and in the West was the effect of the Air Force.

So that is quite correct.

Jackson I remind you of the testimony of the witness Milch, sworn on your behalf, as to a subject on which I have not heard you express yourself. He said:

"I had the impression that already at the time of the occupation of the Rhineland, he, Goering, was worried lest Hitler's policy should lead to war."

Do you remember that?

Goering Yes.

Jackson And was it true or false? True or mistaken, perhaps, I should say.

Goering No, I did not want a war and I thought the best way to avoid a war was to be strongly armed according to the well known adage, "He who has a strong sword has peace."

Jackson Well, you are still of that opinion?

Goering I am of that opinion today, now that I see the entanglements more than ever.

Jackson And it is true, as Milch said, that you were worried that Hitler's policies would lead to war at the time of the occupation of the Rhineland?

Goering Excuse me, I just understood you to ask whether it is also my opinion today that only a nation that is strongly armed can maintain peace. That is what I meant to answer with my last statement.

If you are connecting this question to the statement of Milch, that I was worried lest the policy of the Fuehrer might lead to war, I should like to say that I was worried lest war might come; and if possible I wanted to avoid it, but not in the sense that the policy of the Fuehrer would lead to it, because the Fuehrer also desired to carry out his program by agreements and diplomatic action.

In regard to the occupation of the Rhineland I was somewhat worried at the time about the reactions; all the same, it was necessary.

Jackson And when nothing happened, the next step was Austria?

Goering The one has nothing to do with the other. I never had any misgivings about Austria leading to a war, as I had with the Rhineland occupation, for in the case of the Rhineland occupation I could well imagine that there might be repercussions. But how there could be any repercussions from abroad over the union of two brother nations of purely German blood was not clear to me, especially since Italy, who always pretended that she had a vital interest in a separate Austria, had somewhat changed her ideas. It could not have mattered in the least to England and France, nor could they have had the slightest interest in this union. Therefore I did not see the danger of its leading to a war.

Jackson I ask you just a few questions about Austria. You said that you and Hitler had felt deep regret about the death of Dollfuss, and I ask you if it is not a fact that Hitler put up a plaque in Vienna in honour of the men who murdered Dollfuss, and went and put a wreath on their graves when he was there. Is that a fact? Can you not answer that question with "yes" or "no"?

Goering No, I cannot answer it with either "yes" or "no," if I am to speak the truth according to my oath. I cannot say, "Yes, he did it," because I do not know; I cannot say, "No, he did not do it," because I do not know that either. I want to say that I heard about this event here for the first time.

Jackson Now, in June of 1937, Seyss-Inquart came to you and State Secretary Keppler, and you had some negotiations.

Goering Yes.

Jackson And it was Seyss-Inquart's desire to have an independent Austria, was it not?

Goering As far as I remember, yes.

Jackson And Keppler was the man who was sent by Hitler to Vienna at the time of the Anschluss and who telegraphed to Hitler not to march in, do you recall?

Goering Yes.

Jackson That is the telegram that you characterized as impudent and senseless from the man who was on the spot, and who had negotiated earlier with Seyss-Inquart, do you recall that?

Goering I did not characterize the telegram with this word which has just been translated to me in German, that is "impudent." I said that this telegram could no longer have any influence and was superfluous, because the troops were already on the move and had their order; the thing was already underway.

Jackson You had demanded that Seyss-Inquart be made Chancellor? Is that right?

Goering I did not desire that personally, but it arose out of the circumstance that at that time he was the only man who could assume the Chancellorship because he was already in the Government.

Jackson Now, did Seyss-Inquart become Chancellor of Austria with the understanding that he was to surrender his country to Germany, or did you lead him to believe that he would be independent, have an independent country?

Goering I explained the other day that even at the time when he left by plane the next morning, the Fuehrer himself had still not made up his mind as to whether the union with Austria should not be brought about by means of a joint head of state. I also said that I personally did not consider this solution far-reaching enough and that I was for an absolute, direct, and total Anschluss.

I did not know exactly what Seyss-Inquart's attitude was at this time. Nevertheless I feared that his attitude was rather in the direction of continued separation with co-operation, and did not go as far as my attitude in the direction of a total Anschluss. Therefore I was very satisfied when this total Anschluss crystallized in the course of the day.

Jackson I respectfully submit that the answers are not responsive, and I repeat the question.

Did Seyss-Inquart become Chancellor of Austria with an understanding that he would call in the German troops and surrender Austria to Germany, or did you lead him to believe that he could continue an independent Austria?

Goering Excuse me, but that is a number of questions which I cannot answer simply with "yes" or "no."

If you ask me, "Did Seyss-Inquart become Chancellor according to Hitler's wishes and yours?" -- yes.

If you then ask me, "Did he become Chancellor with the understanding that he should send a telegram for troops to march in?" -- I say, "No," because at the time of the Chancellorship there was no question of his sending us a telegram.

If you ask me, thirdly, "Did he become Chancellor on the understanding that he would be able to maintain an independent Austria?" -- then I have to say again that the final turn of events was not clear in the Fuehrer's mind on that evening.

That is what I tried to explain.

Jackson Is it not true that you suspected that he might want to remain as independent as possible, and that that was one of the reasons why the troops were marched in?

Goering No. Excuse me, there are two questions: I strongly suspected that Seyss-Inquart wanted to be as independent as possible. The sending of troops had nothing at all to do with that suspicion; not a single soldier would have been needed for that. I gave my reasons for the sending of the troops.

Jackson But it was never intimated to Seyss-Inquart that Austria would not remain independent until after -- as you put it -- the Fuehrer and you were in control of Austria's fate? Is that a fact?

Goering That was certainly not told him beforehand by the Fuehrer. As far as I was concerned, it was generally known that I desired it, and I assume that he knew of my attitude.

Jackson Now, you have stated that you then, in conversation with Ribbentrop in London, stressed that no ultimatum had been put to Seyss-Inquart, and you have said that, legally, that was the fact.

Goering I did not say "legally," I said "diplomatically."

President Is that a convenient time to break off?

Jackson Yes, Your Honor.

[The Tribunal adjourned until 19 March 1946 at 1000 hours.]

The Cross Examination of Goering
19th March 1946 - Afternoon

The Tribunal made a break in the cross examination of Goering so the Defence could bring to the stand a witness, Birger Dahlerus. Dahlerus was a Swedish businessman with a wide range of influential contacts in top circles of the United Kingdom and Germany. He had not been available during Goering's defence presentation and the Tribunal had agreed to slot him in at this point.

Dahlerus is a very interesting individual and is remembered for the desperate attempts he made in the last days of peace to prevent the outbreak of war. He had meetings with British Government representatives, and people high in the Nazi Government, including Goering and Hitler himself. His account of those crucial times, *The Last Attempt*, is one of history's great might-have-beens.

Although Dahlerus had been presented as a witness for the defence, his testimony was far from a justification of Goering's actions. The picture it painted of negotiations with the Nazi Government gave the impression that they were using him as no more than a smoke-screen to disguise their preparations. Dahlerus gave evidence until the Tribunal adjourned for lunch.

The examination continued in the afternoon with questions from the counsel for Ribbentrop, Dr Horn, in the interests of his client. It was then the turn of the prosecution to cross examine the witness, and Maxwell-Fyfe took over.

Maxwell-Fyfe's style of questioning was very detailed and focussed. Many of his questions were grounded in *The Last Attempt* and he led Dahlerus step by step through his negotiations, including a revealing session with Hitler himself. Maxwell-Fyfe concluded his questioning by drawing from Dahlerus the admission that 'had I known what I know today, I would have realised that my efforts could not possibly succeed'.

Late in the afternoon, the cross examination of Goering resumed. Jackson must have had a worried evening on March 18th as he thought about that day's questioning, and he would have been further shaken when he tried to start the day by springing a surprise on Goering. He produced the minutes of a meeting of the Reich Defence Council in 1938 in which Goering participated. Goering had previously said he had not attended any meetings of the Council.

The surprise document prompted a wrangle with defence counsels, who did not like surprises and insisted that if such a document were produced in court, they should at least be allowed a copy. Jackson initially resisted – he did not have a spare copy – but the President ruled that documents should be made available promptly, although not necessarily in advance.

Unfortunately for Jackson, the document was not what he believed it to be. It was the record of a speech by Goering to an audience that included members of the council, along with many other people. Goering did not hesitate to point this out, and to make Jackson look foolish.

Jackson was immediately tripped up again by a mis-translation in another document. We can almost hear Goering's glee as he seized on it and explained the reference was not to the liberation of the Rhineland, as Jackson had thought. It referred instead to the clearing of the Rhine river of any unnecessary boats and barges that might interfere with military operations.

The afternoon ended with a bad tempered exchange between Jackson and Goering. Jackson accused Germany of having kept their military mobilisation plans secret (normal practice for all countries) and Goering made the throw-away comment that he did not recall the American Government making their plans public either. Jackson's frustrations bubbled over and he asked the President to treat Goering as 'unresponsive'.

Testimony - Afternoon Session – 19th March 1946

Jackson I call your attention to the testimony which you gave yesterday and ask you if it is correct.

"I think I was Deputy Chairman" -- referring to the Reich Defence

Council -- "I do not even know, I heard about that, but I assure you under my oath, that at no time and at no date did I participate in a single meeting when the Council for the Defence of the Reich was called together as such."

Is that a correct transcription of your testimony?

Goering Yes, I said that in no single.

Jackson That is all. That is all I asked you.

Goering Yes.

Jackson I ask to have your attention called to Document Number 3575-PS (Exhibit Number USA-781) which is the minutes of the Reich Defence Council of 18 November 1938, with you presiding.

I call your attention to the statement that the "meeting consisted solely of a 3-hour lecture by the Field Marshal. No discussion took place."

Is that correct?

[Document 3575-PS was submitted to the defendant.]

Goering I have to read it first, this is the first time I have seen the document.

Jackson You did not know when you testified yesterday that we had this document, did you? Would you kindly answer that question?

Goering I have not seen this document before. I have to look at it first. It says here: "Notes on the session of the Reich Defence Council on 18 November 1938."

The Reich Defence Council, as it was described here, comprised few people. Here there were present, however, all Reich ministers and state secretaries, also the commanders-in-chief of the Army and the Navy, the chiefs of the General Staff, of the three branches of the Armed Forces, Reichsleiter Bormann for the Deputy of the Fuehrer, General Daluege, SS GruppenFuehrer Heydrich, the Reich Labor Fuehrer, the Price Commissioner, the President of the Reich Labor Office, and others.

When I gave my testimony I was thinking only of the Reich Defence Council as such. This is dealing with the Reich Defence Council within the framework of a large assembly. Nevertheless, I was not thinking of that; this concerns, over and beyond the Reich Defence Council, an assembly that was much larger than that provided for under the Reich Defence Council.

Jackson I call your attention to the fact that the "Field Marshal stated it to be the task of the Reich Defence Council to correlate all the forces of the nation for accelerated building up of German armament."

Do you find that?

Goering Yes, I have it now.

Jackson The second paragraph?

Goering Yes.

Jackson Under II, "The Physical Task: The assignment is to raise the level of armament from a current index of 100 to one of 300."

Goering Yes.

Dr Seimers I cannot quite see the reason why it repeatedly happens that the defence does not receive documents that are discussed in Court and that are submitted to the Court. The document now discussed is also not known to us, at least not to me.

During the last few days I have noticed that several times documents were suddenly presented by the prosecution without any effort having been made to inform us of their existence.

Jackson That is perfectly true, and I think every lawyer knows that one of the great questions in this case is credibility, and that if we have, in cross-examination, to submit every document before we can refer to it in cross-examination, after we hear their testimony, the possibilities of useful cross examination are destroyed.

Now, of course, he did not know; and we have had the experience of calling document after document to their attention, always to be met with some explanation, carefully arranged and read here from notes. No defendant has ever had better opportunity to prepare his case than these defendants, and I submit that cross-examination of them should not be destroyed by any requirement that we submit documents in advance.

President Did you wish to say something?

Dr Seimers Yes. I should like to make two points. First, I am entirely agreed if Mr. Justice Jackson wants to make use of the element of surprise. I should merely be thankful if the defence then were also permitted to use the element of surprise. Yet we have been told heretofore that we must show every document we want to submit weeks ahead of time, so that the prosecution has several weeks to form an opinion on it.

Secondly, if the element of surprise is being used, I believe that at least we, as defence counsel, should not be given this surprise at the moment when the document is submitted to the Court and to the witness. I have at this moment neither today's documents nor the documents of the previous days.

President What you have just said is entirely inaccurate. You have never been compelled to disclose any documents which you wished to put to a witness in cross-examination. This is cross-examination and therefore it is perfectly open to counsel for the prosecution to put any document without disclosing it beforehand; just as defence counsel could have put any document to witnesses called on behalf of the prosecution, if they had wished to do so, in cross-examination.

I am sure that if counsel for the defendants wish to re-examine upon any such document as this, a copy of it will be supplied to them for that purpose.

The Tribunal now rules that this document may be put to the witness now.

Dr Seimers Does the defence also have the opportunity, now that it is known to the entire Court, of receiving the document?

President Yes, certainly.

Dr Seimers I should be thankful if I could have a copy now.

Jackson I am frank to say I do not know whether we have adequate copies to furnish them to all the defence counsel now.

President Maybe you have not, but you can let them have one or more copies,

Jackson But I do not think we should furnish copies until the examination with reference to that document is completed, that is to say...

President Yes, Dr. Dix.

Dr Dix I should like to make one request that at least the technical possibilities -- that at least the counsel of these defendants who are being cross-examined also be given the document that is submitted to the defendant, so that they are in a position, just as the Tribunal is, to follow the examination.

If Justice Jackson says that it is his opinion that it would be right for the defence counsel -- in this case my colleague Stahmer -- to receive this document only after the examination -- in this case of Goering -- has ended, I beg earnestly, in the interest of the dignity and prestige of the defence, to take objection to this suggestion of Justice Jackson's. I do not believe that he means by that to insinuate that the defence counsel would be able -- having these documents in its hands at the same time as the Tribunal and at the same time as the witness --

somehow through signs or otherwise to influence the defendant and thereby disturb the cross-examination by Mr. Justice Jackson, or by the prosecutor. Mr. Justice Jackson certainly did not mean that, but one might draw that conclusion.

I therefore make this request: If in the cross-examination, for the purpose of the cross-examination, in view of the altogether justified element of surprise, a document is presented to a witness that at the same time is presented to the Tribunal, that at least a copy of this document be given at the same time to the defence counsel, the defence counsel concerned, either the one who has called the witness or the one whose defendant is in the witness box, so that he can have some idea of what the witness is being confronted with, for Goering could read this document, but Dr. Stahmer could not. In other words, he was not in a position to follow the next part of Mr. Justice Jackson's cross-examination. That is certainly not intended, and would certainly not be fair, and I should therefore like to ask Mr. Justice Jackson to reply to my suggestion, and my application, in order to arrive at an understanding and thereby to relieve the Tribunal of the decision on a question that to me seems self-evident.

President Mr. Justice Jackson, the Tribunal is inclined to think -- the Tribunal certainly thinks -- that you are perfectly right, that there is no necessity, at all, as I have already stated, to disclose the document to the defendants before you use it in cross-examination. But, at the time you use it in cross-examination, is there any objection to handing a copy of it to the counsel for the defendant who is being cross-examined?

Jackson In some instances it is physically impossible because of our situation in reference to these documents. A good many of these documents have come to us very lately. Our photostatic facilities are limited.

President I am not suggesting that you should hand it to all of them, but only to Dr. Stahmer.

Jackson If we have copies, I have no objection to doing that, but if we do not have them in German -- our difficulty has always been to get German copies of these documents.

Dr Dix May I say something else. If it is not possible in German, then it should at least be possible in English, for one English copy will certainly be available. Furthermore, if it is a question of German witnesses, such as Goering, the document will be shown him in

German anyhow; it will certainly be shown the witness in German. I believe that will surely be possible.

[Dr. Siemers approached the lectern.]

President We do not really need to hear more than one counsel on this sort of point. I have already ruled upon your objection, which was that the document should be produced beforehand, but the Tribunal has already ruled that objection should be denied.

Dr Seimers Mr. President, I am sorry. My motion was that the defence counsel should receive these documents at the same time the Tribunal does. I am not of the opinion expressed by Dr. Dix, that only one defence counsel should receive it. If it is a report regarding the Reich Defence Council, then it is a document important to several defendants. One copy is therefore not sufficient, but each defence counsel must have one. I believe that Mr. Justice Jackson…

President But not at this moment. There are, as we all know, the very greatest difficulties in producing all these documents, and extraordinary efforts have been made by the prosecution and the translating division to supply the defendants with documents, and with documents in German, and it is not necessary that every member of the defence counsel have these documents at the time the witness is being cross-examined. I am sure the prosecution will do everything it can to let you have the documents in due course any document that is being used.

In the opinion of the Tribunal it is perfectly sufficient if one copy of the document is supplied to the counsel for the witness who is being cross-examined. As I say, the prosecution will doubtless let you have copies of these documents in due course.

You are appearing for the Defendant Raeder, and the Defendant Raeder, I am afraid, at the present rate will not be in the witness box for some time.

Dr Seimers The result of that is that the defence counsel who is not momentarily concerned, cannot understand the cross-examination. As to the technical question, I ask the Court to consider that I cannot follow Justice Jackson on this technical point. The document is mimeographed by means of a stencil. In mimeographing it makes no difference at all whether 20, 40, 80, or 150 copies are produced. It makes no difference from the point of view of time, except perhaps 4 or 5 minutes. I consider for this reason that one can hardly refer to technical difficulties in this matter.

President Counsel for the prosecution will consider what you say, but no rule has been made by the Tribunal that every document should be supplied to every counsel during cross-examination.

Goering I should like to say again in regard to the document that this is not ...

Jackson May I respectfully ask that the witness be instructed to answer the question and reserve his explanations until his counsel takes him on. Otherwise, this cross-examination cannot successfully be conducted, in the sense of being reasonable in time.

President I have already explained, on several occasions, that it is the duty of defendants when they are in the witness box, and the duty of witnesses, to answer questions directly, if they are capable of being answered directly, in the affirmative or in the negative; and if they have any explanation to make afterwards, they can make it after answering the question directly.

Jackson I call your attention to Item 3, under II, "Finances," reading as follows:

"Very critical situation of the Reich Exchequer. Relief initially through the milliard imposed on the Jews and through profits accruing to the Reich from the Aryanization of Jewish enterprises."

You find that in the minutes, do you not?

Goering Yes, that is there;

Jackson And you find the minutes signed by Woermann, do you not?

Goering No, that is not true. I beg your pardon? Here on the photostat Woermann has signed it, that is not Bormann. I know Bormann's signature well, it is quite different.

Jackson I said Woermann.

Goering Woermann, yes.

Jackson All right, my poor pronunciation. Well, was it not a fact that you set up a working committee under the Reich Defence Council which did meet from time to time and did carry on certain work?

Goering I have already explained recently: That was the committee of departmental chiefs.

Jackson And I call your attention to Document Number EC-405, minutes of a meeting of the Working Committee of the Reich Defence Council, Meeting Number 10.

Goering I understood the President to say before that when I have answered the question, I can add an explanation that seems necessary to me. Now that I have clearly answered your question with regard to the first document, I want to stress once again that this was not a meeting of the close Reich Defence Council but a general calling together of all ministers, state secretaries and numerous other persons. And that I began my statements as follows:

"1. Organization of the Reich Defence Council: The Reich Defence Council was already, by decision of the Cabinet of 1933 and 1934, called into being; but it has never met. Through the Reich Defence Law of 4 September 1938 it was re-established. The Chairman is the Fuehrer, who has appointed General Field Marshal Goering his permanent deputy."

Concerning the Reich Defence Council, about which we have been talking, consisting of Schacht -- or rather -- of the triumvirate -- it is attested here in writing once more, as I have correctly said, that this Council never met. I ask to have the question about the second document repeated, as I have forgotten it.

Jackson You testified that the movement into the Rhineland had not been planned in advance.

Goering Only a short time in advance, I emphasized.

Jackson How long?

Goering As far as I recall, at the most 2 to 3 weeks.

Jackson Now, I call your attention to the minutes of the 10th meeting of the Working Committee of the Reich Defence Council, Document Number EC-405 toward the end of that document, the discussion on 6th month, 26th day of 1935, which reads as follows ...

Goering May I ask what page? This document is very long and is new to me. What page, please, otherwise I shall have to read the whole document.

Jackson Turn to the last paragraph and we will work backwards.

"Commitment to writing of directives for mobilization purposes is permissible only insofar as it is absolutely necessary for the smooth execution of the measures provided for the demilitarized zone. Without exception such material must be kept in safes."

Do you find that part?

Goering This document that has been handed to me contains alternating statements of various individuals, that is, a dialogue. May I ask once more... The last paragraph contains nothing of what you have stated, apparently there must be a difference between the German and English texts. The last paragraph here is altogether irrelevant. Where, please, am I to read in the document?

Jackson Do you find the third paragraph from the end? If my document is correct we have got the same document.

Goering You must tell me who was speaking, for different persons speak here.

[The place in the document was indicated to the defendant.]

Now it has been shown to me. Under the name Jodl; I have to read through it first.

Jackson Do you find this:

"The demilitarized zone requires special treatment. In his speech of 21 May 1935 and in other statements, the Fuehrer and Reich Chancellor declared that the stipulations of the Versailles Treaty and the Locarno Pact regarding the demilitarized zone would be observed."

Do you find this?

Goering Yes.

Jackson And do you find the next paragraph,

"Since at present international entanglements must be avoided under all circumstances, all urgently needed preparations may be made. The preparations as such, or their planning, must be kept in strictest secrecy in the zone itself as well as in the rest of the Reich."

Do you find this?

Goering Yes.

Jackson And you also find,

"These preparations include in particular" -- a) and b) are not important to my present question -- "c) Preparation for the liberation of the Rhine."

Goering Oh, no, here you have made a great mistake. The original phrase -- and this alone is the point in question-is: "c) Preparation for the clearing of the Rhine." It is a purely technical preparation that has nothing at all to do with the liberation of the Rhineland. Here it says, first, mobilization measures for transportation and communications, then "c) Preparation for the clearing of the Rhine," that is, in case of mobilization preparations the Rhine is not to be overburdened with freighters, tugboats, *et cetera*, but the river has to be clear for military measures. Then it continues: "d) Preparation for local defence," *et cetera*. Thus you see, it figures among small quite general, ordinary and usual preparations for mobilization. The phrase used by the prosecution ...

Jackson Mobilization, exactly.

Goering That, if you remember, I stressed clearly in my statement, that in the demilitarized zone general preparations for mobilization were made. I mentioned the purchase of horses, *et cetera*. I wanted only to point out the mistake regarding "clearing of the Rhine," which has nothing to do with the Rhineland, but only with the river.

Jackson Well, those preparations were preparations for armed occupation of the Rhineland, were they not?

Goering No, that is altogether wrong. If Germany had become involved in a war, no matter from which side, let us assume from the East, then mobilization measures would have had to be carried out for security reasons throughout the Reich, in this event even in the demilitarized Rhineland; but not for the purpose of occupation, of liberating the Rhineland.

Jackson You mean the preparations were not military preparations?

Goering Those were general preparations for mobilization, such as every country makes, and not for the purpose of the occupation of the Rhineland.

Jackson But were of a character which had to be kept entirely secret from foreign powers?

Goering I do not think I can recall reading beforehand the publication of the mobilization preparations of the United States.

Jackson Well, I respectfully submit to the Tribunal that this witness is not being responsive, and has not been in his examination, and that it is ...

[The defendant interposed a few words which were not recorded.]

It is perfectly futile to spend our time if we cannot have responsive answers to our questions.

[The defendant interposed a few words which were not recorded.]

We can strike these things out. I do not want to spend time doing that, but this witness, it seems to me, is adopting, and has adopted, in the witness box and in the dock, an arrogant and contemptuous attitude toward the Tribunal which is giving him the trial which he never gave a living soul, nor dead ones either.

I respectfully submit that the witness be instructed to make notes, if he wishes, of his explanations, but that he be required to answer my questions and reserve his explanations for his counsel to bring out.

President I have already laid down the general rule, which is binding upon this defendant as upon other witnesses.

Perhaps we had better adjourn now at this state.

[The Tribunal adjourned until 20 March 1946 at 1000 hours.]

The Cross Examination of Goering
20th March 1946 - Morning

The previous afternoon, Jackson had allowed Goering to get under his skin with his comment about the United States keeping its military information secret, and he chose to start the day with this issue. It is a little difficult to understand what exactly had upset him or even what action he wished the Tribunal to take, and the Tribunal also seems to have been surprised. However, Jackson felt he was 'representing the United States of America' and began to attack the way the Tribunal operated.

This was a peculiar attitude to take. Directly confronting a trial bench is always risky and Jackson, as prosecutor, should have been representing the Tribunal and not the United States.

The only useful upshot of the argument was the Tribunal statement that witnesses should answer questions with a direct yes or no where possible, and afterwards add a short explanation if necessary.

Jackson resumed his cross examination by producing a document, in German and not yet translated, that he hoped would catch Goering out. Jackson did not speak German and consequently had to suffer the indignity of the witness having to explain to him what was in the document and why it did not represent the smoking gun Jackson had hoped for.

The examination moved on to the appalling way in which the German Government treated its Jewish population in the pre-war years. Jackson mentioned the increasingly repressive legislation introduced but without commenting on its morality, and Goering confirmed the legislation in the same non-judgmental way.

Jackson's questioning then reached the events of Kristallnacht when Jewish shops and businesses were attacked and looted by the SA, and Jews themselves killed or attacked. Again, Goering confirmed what had happened, and the questioning moved on to the issue of insurance payments for damage to property.

The difficulty faced by Goering and his colleagues in the aftermath to Kristallnacht is that many of the properties damaged or destroyed had been insured with normal – that is, non-Jewish – insurance companies who would now have to pay for the Nazi's night of chaos.

The discussions over this liability were squalid in the extreme as the German insurance community, with active government support, wriggled out of meeting its obligations.

The remarkable feature of the morning's questioning about the status of Jews in pre-war Germany is that no mention is made of possible illegality. Things were done to Jews that were illegal under German law and should have been seen by the Tribunal as crimes against humanity, but at no point does Jackson attempt to establish this illegality or try to tie Goering to it.

Testimony - Morning Session – 20th March 1946

Jackson If the Tribunal please, the last question which I asked last night referring to mobilization preparations in the Rhineland, as shown in the official transcript, was this: "But of a character which had to be kept entirely secret from foreign powers?" The answer was: "I do not believe I can recall the publication of the preparations of the United States for mobilization."

Now, representing the United States of America, I am confronted with these choices -- to ignore that remark and allow it to stand for people who do not understand our system; or to develop, at considerable expense of time, its falsity; or to answer it in rebuttal. The difficulty arises from this, Your Honor, that if the witness is permitted to volunteer statements in cross-examination there is no opportunity to make objection until they are placed on the record. Of course, if such an answer had been indicated by a question of counsel, as I respectfully submit would be the orderly procedure, there would have been objection; the Tribunal would have been in a position to discharge its duty under the Charter and I would have been in a position to have shortened the case by not having that remark placed.

The Charter in Article 18 provides that the Tribunal shall rule out irrelevant issues and statements of any kind whatsoever. We are squarely confronted with that question; we cannot discharge those duties if the defendant is to volunteer these statements without questions which bring them up. I respectfully submit that, if the ruling of the Tribunal that the defendant may volunteer questions of this kind is to prevail, the control of these proceedings is put in the hands of this defendant, and the United States has been substantially denied its right of cross-examination under the Charter, because cross-examination cannot be effective under this kind of procedure. Since we cannot anticipate, we cannot meet ...

President I quite agree with you that any reference to the United States' secrecy with reference to mobilization is entirely irrelevant, and that the answer ought not to have been made, but the only rule which the Tribunal can lay down as a general rule is the rule -- already laid down -- that the witness must answer if possible "yes" or "no,"   and that he may make such explanations as may be necessary after answering questions directly in that way, and that such explanations must be brief and not be speeches. As far as this particular answer goes, I think it is entirely irrelevant.

Jackson I must, of course, bow to the ruling of the Tribunal, but it is to the second part, I quite recall the admonition of the Court that there shall be answers "yes" or "no."   This witness, of course, pays not the slightest attention to that, and I must say I cannot blame him; he is pursuing his interests. But we have no way of anticipating, and here we are confronted with this statement in the record, because when these statements are volunteered they are in the record before the Tribunal can rule upon them and I have no opportunity to make objections, and the Tribunal have no opportunity to rule. And it puts, as I said before, the control of these proceedings in the hands of the defendant, if he first makes the charges and then puts it up to us to ignore them or answer them by long cross-examination in rebuttal; and I think the specific charge made against the United States of America from the witness stand presents that.

Your Honor now advises the United States that it is an improper answer, but it is in the record and we must deal with it. I respectfully submit that unless we have ...

President What exactly is the motion you are making? Are you asking the Tribunal to strike the answer out of the record?

Jackson Well, no; in a trial of this kind, where propaganda is one of the purposes of the defendant, striking out does no good after the answer is made, and Goering knows that as well as I. The charge has been made against the United States and it is in the record. I am now moving that this witness be instructed that he must answer my questions "yes" or " no" if they permit an answer, and that the explanation be brought out by his counsel in a fashion that will permit us to make objections, if they are irrelevant, and to obtain rulings of the Tribunal, so that the Tribunal can discharge its functions of ruling out irrelevant issues and statements of any kind whatsoever. We must not let the Trial degenerate into a bickering contest between counsel and the witness. That is not what the United States would expect me to participate in. I respectfully suggest that if he can draw any kind of challenge ...

President Are you submitting to the Tribunal that the witness has to answer every question "yes" or "no" and wait until he is re-examined for the purpose of making any explanations at all?

Jackson I think that is the rule of cross-examination under ordinary circumstances. The witness, if the question permits it, must answer, and if there are relevant explanations they should be reserved until later.

Now let me come back to the specific problem I have right here this morning. Here is an answer given which the Tribunal now rules is irrelevant. But we have no opportunity to object to it. The Tribunal had no opportunity to rule upon it. The witness asks, "Did you ever hear of the United States publishing its plan of mobilization?" Of course, we would have objected. The difficulty, is that the Tribunal loses control of these proceedings if the defendant, in a case of this kind where we all know propaganda is one of the purposes of the defendant, is permitted to put his propaganda in, and then we have to meet it afterwards. I really feel that the United States is deprived of the opportunity of the technique of cross-examination if this is the procedure.

President Surely it is making too much of a sentence the witness has said, whether the United States makes its orders for mobilization public or not. Surely that is not a matter of very great importance. Every country keeps certain things secret. Certainly it would be much wiser to ignore a statement of that sort. But as to the general rule, the Tribunal will now consider the matter. I have already laid down what I believe to be the rule, and I think with the assent of the Tribunal, but I will ascertain...

Jackson Let me say that I agree with Your Honor that as far as the United States is concerned we are not worried by anything the witness can say about it -- and we expected plenty. The point is, do we answer these things or leave them, apart from the control of the Trial? And it does seem to me that this is the beginning of this Trial's getting out of hand, if I may say so, if we do not have control of this situation. I trust the Tribunal will pardon my earnestness in presenting this. I think it is a very vital thing.

President I have never heard it suggested that the counsel for the prosecution have to answer every irrelevant observation made in cross-examination.

Jackson That would be true in a private litigation, but I trust the Court is not unaware that outside of this courtroom is a great social question of the revival of Nazism and that one of the purposes of the Defendant Goering -- I think he would be the first to admit -- is to revive and perpetuate it by propaganda from this Trial now in process.

President Yes, Doctor Stahmer?

Dr Stahmer I just wanted to explain the following: An accusation has been made as if we intended to make propaganda here for Nazism, or in some other direction. I do not think this accusation is justified. Neither do I believe that the defendant intended to make an accusation against the United States. I think we have to consider the question that was put to him. That is, it was pointed out to him by the prosecution that this document which was submitted to him was marked "secret." Then he stated that he had never heard that a document of that kind would have been made public in the United States. If instead of the USA he had said any other nation, then the remark would have been considered harmless.

In my opinion the answer was quite justified. The witness should be given the possibility not only to answer "yes" or "no," but to give reasons for his answer, as ruled by the Court.

President Mr. Justice Jackson, the Tribunal considers that the rule which it has laid down is the only possible rule and that the witness must be confined strictly to answering the question directly where the question admits of a direct answer, and that he must not make his explanation before he gives a direct answer; but, after having given a direct answer to any question which admits of a direct answer, he may make a short explanation; and that he is not to be confined simply to making direct answers "yes" or "no" and leaving the explanation until his counsel puts it to him in his re-examination.

As to this particular observation of the defendant, the defendant ought not to have referred to the United States, but it is a matter which I think you might well ignore.

Jackson I shall bow to the ruling, of course.

I wish to make a statement to the Tribunal about one of the documents. At the conclusion of the session yesterday we were considering Document Number EC-405. The Defendant Goering challenged the use of a word which he said should have been translated "clearance" rather than "liberation." We have since had the translation checked and find that the defendant is correct. This document was introduced under Exhibit Number GB-160 on the 9th of January, at Page 2396 of the Tribunal's records (Volume V, Page 28), and since it has already been received in evidence and it is before the Tribunal, we think it incumbent upon the prosecution to make that correction now for the record.

[Turning to the witness.] You stated yesterday that the minutes of the Reich Defence Council with which you were presented were not minutes of a meeting of the Reich Defence Council as such?

Goering Yes, I said that.

Jackson And your testimony, notwithstanding that document, still stands, I take it, that the Reich Defence Council never met?

Goering I said that also, yes.

Jackson I now ask to have you shown a document which has just come into our possession, the minutes of the second session of the Reich Defence Council. I should have said, just come to us for translation. We have not had it translated; we just discovered it among our great collection of documents.

President Could Doctor Stahmer have a copy in English or not?

Jackson We have not even had a chance to get it into English. I do not know what it says except that it is the minutes of their meeting. We have a photostat.

[Turning to the witness.] Are those not the minutes of the second meeting of the Reich Defence Council held on the 23rd of June 1939?

Goering I must read it first.

Jackson I call your attention to the fact that the chairman is Minister President General Field Marshal Goering. You will find that on Page 1.

Goering I have never disputed that. It was fixed by law. This deals with the second Reich Defence Council, not the first one. Besides, I was not present at this meeting; and I point out that on the left is a list of the authorities who took part in the meeting, and in my case it says "Minister President Field Marshal Goering," and on the right, as representative for him, "State Secretary Korner and State Secretary Neumann." But I shall have to look through the document first in order to find out whether I took part personally.

Jackson Does it not say on Page 1, directly under the place of meeting, "Chairman: Minister President Goering"?

Goering Yes. I have to read it first.

Jackson Do you deny the authenticity of those minutes?

Goering I have not looked them through yet.

It seems to be an absolutely authentic copy of the minutes; I admit that. But here again we are dealing with a meeting not, as I said when answering my counsel, of the Reich Defence Council, but of a larger meeting in which many other departments participated; and it is a matter of the second Reich Defence Council, which was set up after 1938, not a secret council such as was the case from 1933-38.

Jackson In other words, in interpreting your testimony, we must understand that, when you say there was no meeting of the Reich Defence Council, you mean only that there were no meetings at which no other people were present?

Goering No, that is not correct. There were two Reich Defence laws concerning the Reich Defence Council which I tried to explain in my statement: the Secret Council of 1933 to 1938, which was not made public, and the Reich Defence Council which was created in 1938 and converted into the Ministerial Council in 1939; the latter held meetings which were in no way confined to its own members.

Jackson Then you say that this was not the Defence Council that met under the ban of secrecy?

Goering The prosecution want me to answer first with "yes" or "no." It is hard to answer this question with "yes" or "no." I assert that the Secret Defence Council, which was not made public and which arose out of a meeting of ministers in 1933, never met. After 1938 a new Reich defence law created a new council. At that time it was clear that our military sovereignty had already been declared. This first council, which the prosecution called the secret one, never met, and the document of yesterday proved that.

Jackson Will you refer to Page 19 of this document, please, and tell me whether one of the very things with which this meeting concerned itself was not the lifting of the secrecy ban from the Reich defence law?

Goering No, that is not the way it reads here. If I may translate it, the last point on the agenda: Consequences resulting from the lifting of the secrecy ban on the Reich defence law and measures to expedite procedures have already been dealt with by a letter from the Reich Defence Committee on 26 June: "Consequences resulting from the lifting of the secrecy ban with a view to expediting written communications."

Jackson You have stated that on the Jewish question, some of the members of the government were more radical than you. Would you state who these were?

Goering Broadly speaking, when we took over the government, we only demanded their removal from political and other leading positions in the State.

Jackson That is not what I asked you.

President That is not a direct answer to the question. The question was that you said some members of the government were more radical toward Jews than you were. Would you tell us which of the members of the government were more radical than you were?

Goering Excuse me, I did not understand the question to mean who were more radical, but in what way they were more radical. If you ask who, then I would say that those were primarily Ministers Goebbels and Himmler.

Jackson Do you also include your co-defendant, Streicher, as more radical than you?

Goering Yes, but he was not a member of the government.

Jackson He was the Gauleiter, was he not, for this very territory in which we are sitting.

Goering That is correct; but he had very little or no influence on government measures.

Jackson What about Heydrich?

Goering Heydrich was subordinate to Himmler. If I said Himmler, I, of course, include Heydrich.

Jackson Heydrich is then included in the list of the more radical ones to whom you refer?

Goering That is right; yes.

Jackson What about Bormann?

Goering It was only during the later years that I observed that Bormann was becoming more radical. I do not know anything about his attitude in the beginning.

Jackson Now, I want to review with you briefly what the prosecution understands to be public acts taken by you in reference to the Jewish question. From the very beginning you regarded the elimination of the Jews from the economic life of Germany as one phase of the Four Year Plan under your jurisdiction, did you not?

Goering The elimination, yes; that is partly correct. The elimination as far as the large industries were concerned, because there were continual disturbances due to the fact that there were large industries, also armament industries, still partly under Jewish directors, or with Jewish shareholders, and that gave rise to a certain anxiety among the lower ranks.

Jackson Now, do I understand that you want the Tribunal to believe that all you were concerned about was the big Jewish enterprises? That is the way you want to be understood?

Goering I was not at first disturbed by the small stores. They did not come into the Four Year Plan.

Jackson When did you become disturbed by the small stores?

Goering When trade had to be limited, it was pointed out that this could be done first by closing the Jewish stores.

Jackson Now, let us go through the public acts which you performed on the Jewish question. First, did you proclaim the Nuremberg Laws?

Goering As President of the Reichstag, yes. I have already stated that.

Jackson What date was that?

Goering 1935, I believe; here in Nuremberg, in September.

Jackson That was the beginning of the legal measures taken against the Jews, was it not?

Goering That was a legal measure.

Jackson That was the first of the legal measures taken by your government against the Jews, was it not?

Goering No, I believe the removal from office was before.

Jackson When was that?

Goering I could not state the exact date, but I believe that happened in 1933.

Jackson Then on the first day of December 1936, you promulgated an act making it a death penalty for Germans to transfer property abroad or leave it abroad; the property of a culprit to be forfeited to the State, and the People's Court given jurisdiction to prosecute, did you not?

Goering That is correct; the "Decree Governing Restriction on Foreign Currency." That is to say, whoever had an account in a foreign country without permission of the government.

Jackson Then, your third public act was on 22 April 1938 when you published penalties for veiling the character of a Jewish enterprise within the Reich, was it not?

Goering Yes.

Jackson Then on 28 July 1939, you, Hermann Goering, published certain prescriptions on the competence of the courts to handle those matters by the decree, did you not?

Goering Please, would you kindly read the law to me? I cannot recall it.

Jackson I will not take time reading it. Do you deny that you published the *Reichsgesetzblatt* law, 1939, found on Page 1370, referring to the competence of the courts to handle penalties against Jews? If you do not remember, say so.

Goering Yes, I say that I cannot remember the law. If it is in the *Reichsgesetzblatt* and bears my name, then, of course, it is so; but I do not remember the contents.

Jackson Now, on 26 April 1938 you, under the Four Year Plan, published a decree providing for the registration of Jewish property and provided that Jews inside and outside Germany must register their property, did you not?

Goering I assume so. I no longer remember it, but if you have the decree there, and if it is signed by me, there cannot be any doubt.

Jackson On 26 April 1938 you published a decree under the Four Year Plan, did you not, that all acts of disposal of Jewish enterprises required the permission of the authorities?

Goering That I remember.

Jackson Then you published on 12 November 1938 a decree, also under the Four Year Plan, imposing a fine of a billion marks for atonement on all Jews?

Goering I have already explained that all these decrees at that time were signed by me, and I assume responsibility for them.

Jackson Well, I am asking you if you did not sign that particular decree? I am going to ask you some further questions about it later.

Goering Yes.

Jackson Then on the 12th of November 1938, you also signed a decree that, under the Four Year Plan, all damage caused to Jewish property by the riots of 1938 must be repaired immediately by the Jews, and at their own expense; and their insurance claims were forfeited to the Reich. Did you personally sign that law?

Goering I did sign a similar law. Whether it was exactly the same as you have just read, I could not say.

Jackson You do not disagree that that was the substance of the law, do you?

Goering No.

Jackson And on the 12th of November 1938, did you not also personally sign a decree, also under the Four Year Plan, that Jews may not own retail stores, or engage independently in handicrafts or offer goods, or services, for sale at markets, fairs, or exhibitions; or act as leaders of enterprises or as members of co-operatives? Do you recall all of that?

Goering Yes. Those are all parts of the decrees for the elimination of Jewry from economic life.

Jackson Then, on the 21st of February 1939, you personally signed a decree, did you not, that the Jews must surrender all objects of precious metals and jewels purchased, to the public office within 2 weeks?

Goering I do not remember that, but without doubt, that is correct.

Jackson I refer to Volume I of the *Reichsgesetzblatt*, 1939, Page 282. You have no recollection of that?

Goering I have not the *Reichsgesetzblatt* in front of me now, but if there is a decree in the *Reichsgesetzblatt*, or a law signed with my name, then I signed that law and decreed it.

Jackson Did you not also, on the 3rd of March 1939, sign a further decree concerning the period within which items of jewellery must be surrendered by Jews -- *Reichsgesetzblatt*, Volume 1, 1939, Page 387?

Goering I assume that was the decree for the execution of the decree for surrender previously mentioned. A law sometimes requires regulations and decrees for execution consequent upon the law. Taken together, this is one single measure.

Jackson Did you not also sign personally a decree under the Four Year Plan, of the 17th of September 1940, ordering the sequestration of Jewish property in Poland?

Goering Yes, as I stated before, in that part of Poland which, I may say, as an old German province, was to return to Germany.

Jackson Did you not also, on the 30th day of November 1940, personally sign a decree which provided that the Jews should receive no compensation for damages caused by enemy attacks or by German forces, and did you not sign that in the capacity of President of the Reich Defence Council? I refer to the *Reichsgesetzblatt*, Volume 1, 1940, Page 1547.

Goering If you have it there before you, then it must be correct.

Jackson You have no recollection of that?

Goering Not of all the separate laws and decrees. That is impossible.

Jackson Then, it was you, was it not, who signed, on the 31st day of July 1941, a decree asking Himmler, and the Chief of Security Police and the SS GruppenFuehrer Heydrich to make the plans for the complete solution of the Jewish question?

Goering No, that is not correct. I know that decree very well.

Jackson I ask to have you shown Document 710, Exhibit Number USA-509.

President Is that 710-PS?

Jackson 710-PS, Your Honor.

[Turning to the witness.] That document is signed by you, is it not?

Goering That is correct.

Jackson And it is addressed to the Chief of the Security Police and the Security Service, and to SS GruppenFuehrer Heydrich, isn't it?

Goering That is also correct.

Jackson I am not certain whether the entire thing has been read into the record, but I think it should be; and, that we may have no difficulty about the translation of this, you correct me if I am wrong:

"Completing the task that was assigned to you on the 24th of January 1939..."

Goering Here is a mistake already. It says: "Complementing" not "completing" the task which has been assigned to you.

Jackson Very well, I will accept that.

"... which dealt with arriving at a thorough furtherance of emigration and evacuation, a solution of the Jewish problem, as advantageously as possible, I hereby charge you with making all necessary preparations in regard to organizational and financial matters for bringing about a complete solution of the Jewish question in the German sphere of influence in Europe."

Am I correct so far?

Goering No, that is in no way correctly translated.

Jackson Give us your translation of it?

Goering May I read it as it is written here?

"Complementing the task which was conferred upon you already on 24 January 1939, to solve the Jewish problem by means of emigration and evacuation in the best possible way according to present conditions, I charge you herewith to make all necessary preparations as regards organizational, factual, and material matters ..."

Now comes the decisive word which has been mistranslated: "for a total solution," not "for a final solution."

"... for a total solution of the Jewish question within the area of German influence in Europe. Should these come within the competence of other governmental departments, then such departments are to co-operate.

"I charge you further to submit to me as soon as possible a general plan showing the organizational and material measures for reaching the desired total solution of the Jewish question.... Complementing the task assigned to you on 24 January 1939 ..."

That was at a time when there was no war or prospect of a war.

Jackson Now are you reporting the instrument or are you making an explanation?

Goering I wanted to add an explanation to the quotation and just to point out the date.

Jackson Yes. Well, I just did not want it to appear that it was a part of the instrument. The last that is contained in the instrument is:

"I charge you furthermore to send me, before long, an overall plan concerning the organizational, factual, and material measures necessary for the accomplishment of the desired solution of the Jewish question."

Is that not a substantially accurate translation of your order to Heydrich and Himmler?

Goering To Heydrich and the other government departments which had anything to do with it. That can be seen from the first part of the letter, the last sentence.

Jackson Let us have no misunderstanding about this translation now. This letter was directed to the Chief of the Security Police and the Security Service, and SS GruppenFuehrer Heydrich. We are right about that, are we not?

Goering That is correct, but I have to make an explanation in connection with that.

Jackson All right.

Goering The reason I sent this letter to him was that, by the decree of 24 January 1939, Heydrich, or it may have been Himmler, had been given the task of dealing with the emigration of the Jews. Therefore this was the government department concerned, and it was to the department which had been given the task that I had to apply concerning all material and economic matters arising there from.

Jackson Yes. And you ordered all other governmental agencies to co-operate with the Security Police and the SS in the final solution of the Jewish question, did you not?

Goering There is nothing about the SS here, only about the Sicherheitspolizei, a governmental agency. The fact that Heydrich was SS GruppenFuehrer had no direct bearing on it, because it was sent to the Chief of the Security Police -- mentioning his rank as SS GruppenFuehrer Heydrich.

Jackson And mentioning his rank in the SS was just superfluous and has nothing to do with the case?

Goering I have to explain that. For instance, if I write to the Commander-in-Chief of the Army, then I write: "To the Commander-in-Chief of the Army, Colonel General or Field Marshal Von Brauchitsch." And if I write to the Chief of the Security Police, then I must address it: "To the Chief of the Security Police, SS GruppenFuehrer Heydrich." That was his rank and his title. However, that does not mean that the SS had anything to do with it.

Jackson Now, at the time that you issued this order you had received complete reports as to the 1938 riots and Heydrich's part in them, hadn't you?

Goering At that time I had no knowledge of Heydrich's part in the riots -- only Heydrich's report on the riots, for which I had asked.

Jackson All right. Now we will show you Document Number 3058-PS, in evidence as Exhibit Number USA-508.

[Document 3058-PS was submitted to the witness.]

That is the report written by Heydrich which you say you had received, and it is dated 11 November 1938, is it not?

Goering That is correct.

Jackson And it recited to you the looting of Jewish shops, the arrest of 174 persons for looting, the destruction of 815 shops, 171 dwellings set on fire or destroyed, and that this indicated only a fraction of the actual damage caused; 191 synagogues were set on fire, and another 76 completely destroyed; in addition, 11 parish halls, cemetery chapels, and similar buildings were set on fire, and 3 more completely destroyed; 20,000 Jews were arrested; also, 7 Aryans and 3 foreigners -- the latter were arrested for their own safety; 36 deaths were reported, and the seriously injured were also numbered at 36. Those killed and injured are Jews. One Jew is still missing. The Jews killed include 1 Polish national and those injured include 2 Poles.

You had that report on or about the 11th day of November 1938, did you not?

Goering That is correct. That is the report mentioned by me and which I had asked the police to supply, because I wanted to know what had happened up to then.

Jackson Exactly. And the note was made at the top of it, "The General Field Marshal has been informed and no steps are to be taken." Was it not?

Goering That is not quite correct. It says here, "General Field Marshal has taken note. No steps are to be taken by any other office," because I myself wanted to take them.

Jackson Now, you know that that is not true, do you not, that steps were to be taken by some other office? I put it to you squarely whether you are telling this Tribunal the truth when you say that no steps were to be taken by anyone else.

Goering This is a note by my staff department, that nothing was to be done by that quarter, because I said I was going to deal with it personally. In fact I went straight to the Fuehrer with this report.

Jackson All right. Did you receive a report from the Chief Party Judge of the Nazi Party, dated Munich, the 13th of February 1939, concerning the proceedings taken by the Party in these matters?

Goering That is correct. I received that report much later.

Jackson And at the time you appointed -- I withdraw the question. It is obvious from the dates of the documents. You acknowledged the receipt of that document, did you not, to Party member Buch?

Goering That is also correct.

Jackson And the only proceedings that were taken about these riots were those taken by the Party Court, were they not?

Goering Not quite; some were brought before the law courts. That is in the report also.

Jackson I ask that he be shown the report, which is Document 3063-PS. It is not in evidence. Since the document apparently has not been brought here, I will ask you from your recollection.

Goering I know it fairly well.

Jackson I thought so.

Goering No, because it has been submitted to me before, here.

Jackson Yes, it has not been kept from you. Now, in the first place, the Party Court reported that it was probably understood -- I quote -- "by all of the Party leaders present, from oral instructions of the Reich Propaganda Director, that the Party should not appear outwardly as the originator of the demonstrations, but in reality should organize and execute them." Was that the report of the Party Court?

Goering The Party Court, as a result of its investigation, established that the Propaganda Chief, Dr. Goebbels, had given these directives. May I ask, if we are dealing with a report dated March or maybe April?

Jackson The 13th of February 1939, is the date.

Goering Yes, that is correct; that is the result of investigations after the incidents.

Jackson That is right. Now, as a result of the riots, did the Court, the Party Court, not also report this to you: that the Supreme Party Court has reserved itself the right to investigate the killings, also the severe mistreatment and moral crimes and will request the Fuehrer to drop proceedings against any person whom the Party Court did not find guilty of excesses?

Goering That is correct.

Jackson And the Party Court was made up of Gauleiter and Group Leaders of the Party?

Goering The Party Court changed. I cannot say just now, without having the document, who made up the Party Court at that time. I see that I am being given the document.

Jackson I call your attention to Page 4, toward the bottom, where the report says, "Gauleiter and Group Leaders of the branches served as jurors at the trials and decisions."

Goering Yes, it was a matter of course that the jurors of the Party

Court were always taken from these categories according to their importance. I wanted only to say I did not know which persons were taking part here.

Jackson Now, the Party Court found five persons guilty of offenses, did they not? Number 1, a Party member, was guilty of a moral crime and race violation and he was expelled. Is that right?

Goering And turned over to the penal court. That is what it says in the last sentence.

Jackson That is right. Another Party member, Case Number 2, was suspected of race violation and expelled from the Nazi Party.

Goering Expelled for suspected race violation and theft, and turned over to the ordinary court.

Jackson Yes; and Number 2, Gustav, was expelled from the Party and SA for theft. Right?

Goering You are at Number 3?

Jackson I have Number 2, Gustav, the first name mentioned.

Goering Gustav is the first name - Gerstner -- yes, for theft, also turned over to the ordinary court for suspected race violation.

Jackson Now, Number 3 dealt with two expulsions of Party members on the grounds of moral crimes against a Jewess, and they are now held in protective custody. Right?

Goering Expelled from the NSDAP and taken into protective custody; they were also turned over to the civil court later. I know that very well.

Jackson Now, we come to Cases 4 and 5, the first of which was a man, a Party member and SA member, who was reprimanded and declared unfit to hold office for 3 years because of a disciplinary offense, namely, for killing the Jewish couple Selig, contrary to order. Is that right?

Goering That is correct.

Jackson And in the last of these cases the offender was reprimanded and declared unfit to hold office for 3 years for shooting a 16-year-old Jew, contrary to orders after completion of the drive. Is that right?

Goering That is correct.

Jackson We now come to the cases of the killing of Jews, where proceedings were suspended or minor punishments pronounced. I will not go through those in detail, but it is a fact that only minor punishments were pronounced by the Supreme Court of the Party for the killing of Jews, were they not?

Goering Yes, that is correct.

Jackson I now ask you to turn to Page 8.

Goering One moment please.

Jackson I call your attention to the language in regard to Cases 3 to 16.

Goering Which page, please?

Jackson Nine, I believe it is. The Supreme Party Court asks the Fuehrer to quash the proceedings in the State criminal courts.

Goering To quash them, to beat them down, that does not mean suppress. A penal proceeding can be "niedergeschlagen." In Germany that is a different thing from "suppress."

Jackson Well, you give us your version of it and tell us what it is. What does beating down a proceeding mean? Does it mean that it has ended?

Goering That is what it means, but it can only be ordered by an office which has authority to do it; that is to say, the Fuehrer can at any time "beat down" a proceeding by way of an amnesty. The Cabinet could at any time pass a resolution to "beat down" a proceeding -- suppressing it would have been illegal. In Germany, "niedergeschlagen" is a legal term meaning "to suspend."

Jackson And one further question. It was also reported to you, was it not, in that report -- I refer to Page 11: "The public down to the last man realize that political drives, like those of 9 November, were organized and directed by the Party, whether this is admitted or not. When all the synagogues burned down in one night, it must have been organized in some way and can only have been organized by the Party."

That also was in the report of the Supreme Party Court, was it not?

Goering I have not found it yet. It is not the same page as mine.

Jackson Let us find it and not have any mistake about it. Page 11. I should think it would be at the very bottom of Page 10, perhaps, where it starts.

Goering Yes, I have just found it.

Jackson Did I give a reasonably correct translation of it?

Goering That is correct.

President Would that be a convenient time to break off? Before we break off, will you offer in evidence these documents that you have been putting to the witness? Those which are not already in evidence?

Jackson Yes, they should be, Your Honor, I will do that.

President I think Document 3575-PS may have been offered yesterday, but not strictly offered in evidence; and Document 3063-PS today; and one other document the number of which I have not got.

Jackson I appreciate very much your calling my attention to it.

[A recess was taken.]

Jackson *[Turning to the witness.]* Now, the *Volkischer Beobachter* of the 12th of March 1933 quotes a speech of yours delivered at Essen on the 11th of March 1933, including the following -- and I refresh your recollection by calling it to your attention:

"I am told that I must employ the police. Certainly I shall employ the police, and quite ruthlessly, whenever the German people are hurt; but I refuse the notion that the police are protective troops for Jewish stores. No, the police protect whoever comes into Germany legitimately, but it does not exist for the purpose of protecting Jewish usurers."

Did you say that?

Goering When did you say that was?

Jackson Did you say that on the 11th of March 1933 in a speech at Essen, either that or that in substance?

Goering That is correct, but the circumstances were different. Before I answer, I would like to ask whether you have finished with the document in the book that was submitted to me previously. I gave no explanation and will ask my counsel to have me questioned later in regard to that document.

Jackson That is satisfactory.

After the riots of November 9th and 10th, you have testified that you called a meeting on the 12th of November and ordered all officials concerned to be present, and that the Fuehrer had insisted on Goebbels being present.

Goering Yes, all chiefs of the economic departments.

Jackson Could you tell us who was there in addition to yourself and Goebbels?

Goering As far as I recall, the following were there for the purpose of reporting: The Chief of the Secret State Police, concerning the events, the Minister of Economy, the Minister of Finance, the Minister of the Interior...

Jackson Will you please state their names so that there will not be any mistake about who was there at that time.

Goering I can quote only from memory. There were present to draw up a report: The leader of the Secret State Police in Berlin, Heydrich; the Minister of the Interior, Dr. Frick; Dr. Goebbels you have mentioned already; the then Minister of Economy, Funk, was there; the Finance Minister, Count Schwerin von Krosigk; and Fischbock from Austria.

Those are the only names I can recall at present, but there may have been a few others there too.

Jackson Part of the time, Hilgard, representing the insurance companies, was also present, was he not?

Goering He was summoned and waited there. His views were asked on special questions.

Jackson Now, you have been shown the stenographic minutes of that meeting which are in evidence as Exhibit Number USA-261, being Document Number 1816-PS, have you not, in your interrogation?

Goering Yes.

Jackson I will ask that they be shown to you, and now, so that we may have no misunderstanding about the translations.

You opened the meeting with this statement. I will read it: "Gentlemen..." I think perhaps we had better be clear about which meeting it was. This is the meeting held on the 12th day of November 1938 at the office of the Reich Air Ministry. That is correct, is it not?

Goering Yes, that is correct.

Jackson You opened the meeting:

"Gentlemen, today's meeting is of a decisive nature. I have received a letter written on the Fuehrer's orders by the Stabsleiter of the Fuehrer's Deputy, Bormann, requesting that the Jewish question be now, once and for all, co-ordinated and solved one way or another."

Is that correct?

Goering Yes, that is correct.

Jackson Further down, I find this:

"Gentlemen, I have had enough of these demonstrations. They do not harm the Jews, but finally devolve on me, the highest authority for the German economy. If today a Jewish shop is destroyed, if goods are thrown into the street, the insurance company will pay the Jew for the damages so that he does not suffer any damage at all. Furthermore, consumer goods, goods belonging to the people, are destroyed. If, in the future, demonstrations occur -- and on occasion they may be necessary -- then I ask that they be so directed that we do not cut our own throats."

Am I correct?

Goering Yes, quite correct.

Jackson Skipping two or three paragraphs, I come to this ...

Goering But the supplement has been omitted.

Jackson Well, you can supplement it any way you want to.

Goering:

"...then I ask that they be so directed that we do not cut our own throats. For it is absurd to empty and set fire to a Jewish store, when a German insurance company has to cover the damage, and the goods which I sorely need are burned. I might as well take and burn the raw materials when they come in."

Jackson That is right. You read any part of it that you want to as we go along, in addition to what I read.

"I am not going to tolerate a situation in which the German insurance companies are the ones to suffer. To prevent this, I will use my authority and issue a decree. In this, of course, I ask for the support of the competent, government agencies, so that everything shall be settled properly and the insurance companies will not be the ones who suffer.

"But another problem immediately emerges: It may be that these insurance companies have re-insurance in foreign countries. If there are such re-insurances, I would not want to give them up, because they bring in foreign exchange. The matter must be looked into. For that reason, I have asked Mr. Hilgard from the insurance company to attend, since he is best qualified to tell us to what extent the insurance companies are covered by re-insurance against such damage. I would not want to give this up under any circumstances."

Is that correct?

Goering That is absolutely correct.

Jackson "I do not want to leave any doubt, gentlemen, as to the purpose of today's meeting. We have not come together merely to talk again, but to make decisions; and I earnestly ask the competent departments to take trenchant measures for the Aryanizing of German economy and to submit them to me as far as is necessary."

Goering That is correct.

Jackson I then skip a considerable portion, unless there is more that you wish to put in, and come to this statement:

"The State Trustee will estimate the value of the business and decide what amount the Jew shall receive. Naturally, this amount is to be fixed as low as possible. The State Trustee will then transfer the business to Aryan ownership. The aim is thus accomplished, inasmuch as the business is transferred to the right ownership and its goodwill and balance sheet remain unimpaired.

"Then the difficulties begin. It is easily understandable that attempts will be made on a large scale to get Party members into all these stores and thus give them some compensation. I have witnessed terrible things in the past; little chauffeurs of Gauleiter have profited so much by these transactions that they have raked in half a million. You gentlemen know it. Is that correct?"

And they assented.

Goering Yes, I said that.

Jackson Would you care to read anything further in connection with that?

Goering Perhaps only the next sentence:

"These are, of course, things which are not permissible, and I shall not hesitate to deal ruthlessly with such underhand dealings. If a prominent person is involved I shall go straight to the Fuehrer and report these dirty tricks quite impartially."

Jackson That is, if any individual was attempting to profit by Jewish possessions -- is that what you meant?

Goering By Aryanization.

Jackson I will quote another portion:

"In other words, it must be an ordinary business transaction. One sells his business and another buys it. If there are Party members among the would-be purchasers, they are to be given preference if they fulfil the same conditions. First of all should come those who have suffered damage. After that, preference should be given on grounds of Party membership."

I will skip a line or two:

"This Party member should have a chance to buy the business for as cheap a price as possible. In such a case, the State will not receive the full price, but only the amount the Jew received."

Is that correct?

Goering Just a moment, please, I believe you skipped something.

Jackson Yes, we did. If you want to put it in, you may read it.

Goering No, I want to put it quite briefly, so that it will not take too long. I said what you have already said, that all things being equal, the Party member is to be given preference, the first on the list being the member who suffered prejudice by having his business license cancelled because he was a Party member. Then follows the paragraph which you read and which is correct.

Jackson Now, you then speak at considerable length of the method by which you intended to Aryanize Jewish businesses, is that right?

Goering Yes.

Jackson And then you take up the Aryanization of Jewish factories.

Goering Yes.

Jackson You speak of the smaller factories first.

Goering Yes.

Jackson Have you found the place where you speak of the factories?

Goering Yes, I have found it.

Jackson I quote.

"Now the factories. With regard to the smaller and medium-sized ones, two things will have to be made clear: First, which are the factories for which I have no use, and which can be shut-down? Could they not be put to another use? If not, then these factories are to be pulled down. Second, if the factory should be needed, it will be turned over to Aryans in the same manner as the stores."

That is correct, isn't it?

Goering Yes.

Jackson Do you care to say any more on that subject?

Goering No, those are the basic elements for the laws.

Jackson Now, I call your attention to the second paragraph, starting, "Take now the larger factories." Do you find that?

Goering Yes.

Jackson Dealing with the larger factories, do you not say the solution is very simple, that the factory can be compensated in the same manner as the stores, that is, at a rate which we shall determine, and the Trustee shall take over the Jew's interest, as well as his shares, and in turn sell or transfer them to the State as he thinks fit.

Goering That means anyone who has any interest in the factories will receive compensation, according to the scale laid down by us.

Jackson And the reparation will be turned over to the State Trustee, will it not?

Goering Yes, to the State Trustee. The matter was simply this: The Jew relinquished his ownership and received bonds. That was to be settled by the Trustee through 3 percent bonds.

Jackson Well, we will pass on to where you deal with the foreign Jews, do you recall that?

Goering Yes.

Jackson At that point a representative of the Foreign Office claimed the right to participate on behalf of the Foreign Minister, is that right?

Goering Yes.

Jackson Well, now, we will pass on to the point of the conversation between yourself and Heydrich.

Goering Just a moment, please. Part of the minutes are missing. All right. I have found the place where Heydrich is mentioned for the first time.

Jackson You inquired how many synagogues were actually burned, and Heydrich replied, "Altogether there were 101 synagogues destroyed by fire, 76 synagogues demolished, and 7,500 stores destroyed in the Reich." Have I quoted that correctly?

Goering Yes.

Jackson Well, then Dr. Goebbels interposed, "I am of the opinion that this is our chance to dissolve the synagogues." And then you have a discussion about the dissolving of the synagogues, have you not?

Goering By Dr. Goebbels, yes.

Jackson Then, Dr. Goebbels raised the question of Jews travelling in railway trains?

Goering Yes.

Jackson Let me know if I quote correctly the dialogue between you and Dr. Goebbels on that subject. Dr. Goebbels said:

"Furthermore, I advocate that Jews be banned from all public places where they might cause provocation. It is still possible for a Jew to share a sleeper with a German. Therefore, the Reich Ministry of Transport must issue a decree ordering that there shall be separate compartments for Jews. If this compartment is full, then the Jews cannot claim a seat. They can only be given separate compartments after all Germans have secured seats. They must not mix with the Germans; if there is no more room, they will have to stand in the corridor."

Is that right?

Goering Yes, that is correct.

Jackson "Goering: I think it would be more sensible to give them separate compartments.

"Goebbels: Not if the train is overcrowded.

"Goering: Just a moment. There will be only one Jewish coach. If that is filled up the other Jews will have to stay at home.

"Goebbels: But suppose there are not many Jews going, let us say, on the long-distance express train to Munich. Suppose there are two Jews on the train, and the other compartments are overcrowded; these two Jews would then have a compartment to themselves. Therefore, the decree must state, Jews may claim a seat only after all Germans have secured a seat.

"Goering: I would give the Jews one coach or one compartment, and should a case such as you mention arise, and the train be overcrowded, believe me, we will not need a law. He will be kicked out all right, and will have to sit alone in the toilet all the way."

Is that correct?

Goering Yes. I was getting irritated when Goebbels came with his small details when important laws were being discussed. I refused to do anything. I issued no decrees or laws in this connection. Of course, today, it is very pleasant for the prosecution to bring it up, but I wish to state that it was a very lively meeting at which Goebbels made demands which were quite outside the economic sphere, and I used these expressions to give vent to my feelings.

Jackson Then Goebbels, who felt very strongly about these things, said that Jews should stand in the corridor, and you said that they would have to sit in the toilet. That is the way you said it?

Goering No, it is not. I said that they should have a special compartment; and when Goebbels still was not satisfied, and harped on it, I finally told him, "I do not need a law. He can either sit in the toilet or leave the train." These are utterances made in this connection which, however, have nothing to do with the world-wide importance of the great conflict.

Jackson Let us go down to where Goebbels brings up the subject of the German forests.

Goering Just a moment. Yes. It starts where Goebbels asked for a decree which would prevent Jews from going to German holiday resorts. To which I replied "Give them their own." And then he suggested that it would have to be considered whether we should give them their own resorts, or place some German bathing places at their disposal, but not the best ones so that people might say: "You allow the Jews to get fit by using our bathing resorts." The question must also be considered whether it was necessary to forbid the Jews to go into the German forests. Herds of Jews are today running around in Grunewald; that is a constant provocation -- and so on. Then when he broke in again, I replied very sharply, "It would be better to put a certain part of the forest at the disposal of the Jews," as he wanted them out of the whole of the forests. Then I made the remark which seems to be of so much interest.

Jackson Let us have that remark. Is it not correct, you did state:

"We will give the Jews a certain part of the forest, and Alpers will see to it that the various animals, which are damnably like the Jews -- the elk too has a hooked nose -- go into the Jewish enclosure and settle down among them."

Is that what you said?

Goering Yes, I said it, but it should be linked up with the whole atmosphere of the meeting. Goebbels comes back on it again in the next sentence and says he considers my attitude provoking. I too can say I was provoked by his insistence on unimportant things, when such far-reaching and decisive matters were being discussed.

Jackson Now, you come to the point where you ask Mr. Hilgard from the insurance company to come in. Can you find that?

Goering Yes.

Jackson Then you made a statement Mr. Hilgard when he came in.

"The position is as follows: Because of the justified anger of the people against the Jews, the Reich has suffered a certain amount of damage. Windows have been broken, goods damaged, and people hurt; synagogues have been burned, and so forth, I suppose many of the Jews are also insured against damage committed by public disorder?

"Hilgard: Yes.

"Goering: If that is so, the following situation arises. The people in their justified anger meant to harm the Jews, but it is the German insurance companies which have to compensate the Jews for the damage. The thing is simple enough. I have only to issue a decree to the effect that damage resulting from these riots shall not have to be paid by the insurance companies."

Is that what you said?

Goering Yes, I said all that.

Jackson Hilgard then outlined three kinds of insurance. He pointed out that at least as far as plate glass insurance was concerned, the majority of the sufferers were Aryans who owned buildings and that, as a rule, the Jews only rented them. Is that right?

Goering Yes, those are the details of the discussion.

Jackson And Hilgard said:

"May I draw your attention to the following facts: Plate glass is not manufactured by the Bohemian glass industry, but is entirely in the hands of the Belgian glass industry. In my estimation the damage amounts to 6 millions; that is to say, under the insurance policies, we shall have to pay the owners, who for the most part are Aryans, about 6 millions compensation for the glass."

President Mr. Justice Jackson, before you pass from that page, in the third paragraph, just for the sake of accuracy, it appears that the name "Mr. Hilgard" is wrongly placed, does it not, because he seems both to put the question and to answer it.

Jackson Well, I think that is ...

President Probably the Defendant Goering put the question. It is the third paragraph on my page.

Jackson I take the minutes to read that when Hilgard appeared, Goering addressed him as "Mr. Hilgard."

President Yes, I see.

Jackson But it is correct, as Your Honor suggests.

Goering I wish to point out what was said before concerning the broken glass. Goebbels said: "The Jews must pay for the damage," and I said, "It is no use, we have no raw material, it is all foreign glass. That will require foreign currency. It is like asking for the moon." Then Hilgard comes with the discussions just mentioned.

Jackson Yes, and Hilgard pointed out that:

"Incidentally the amount of damage equals about half a year's production of the whole of the Belgian glass industry. We believe that the manufacturers will take 6 months to deliver the glass."

Do you recall that?

Goering Yes.

Jackson Well, passing down, you come to a point at which Hilgard tells you about a store on Unter den Linden which was attacked. Can you find that?

Goering He said, "The biggest incident is the case of Margraf, Unter den Linden." Isn't that so?

Jackson That is right.

Goering Yes.

Jackson "The damage reported to us amounts to 1,700,000 because the store was completely ransacked." Is that right?

Goering Yes.

Jackson "Goering: Daluege and Heydrich, you must get me these jewels by large-scale raids." Is that the order you gave?

Goering Yes, of course, so that the stolen goods should be brought back.

Jackson Brought back to you, not to the Jews?

Goering Not to me personally, I beg your pardon, that is quite clear.

Jackson Brought back to the State -- you did not intend to return them to the Jews?

Goering It does not say that here. The main thing is, that they should be brought back.

Jackson "We are trying to get the loot back," as Heydrich put it, is that right? And you added, "And the jewels?"

Goering If a large jewellery shop is plundered, something must be done about it because with these valuables a great deal of trouble could be caused. Therefore, I ordered raids to be carried out to have these things, as well as other stolen goods, brought back. When a business was Aryanized, its stock was also transferred to the new owner. The main point, however, was that action should be taken against those who had stolen and plundered, and in fact 150 had already been arrested.

Jackson And Heydrich went on to report on the method of these raids after you reminded him to bring back, to get the jewels.

"It is difficult to say. Some of the articles were thrown into the street and picked up. The same happened with the furriers. For example, in the Friedrichstrasse in the district of Police Station C. There the crowd naturally rushed to pick up mink and skunk furs, *et cetera*. It will be very difficult to recover them. Even children filled their pockets just for the fun of the thing. It is suggested that the Hitler

Youth should not be employed on such actions without the Party's consent. Such things are very easily destroyed."

Goering Yes, so it says.

Jackson And Daluege then suggests:

"The Party should issue an order to the effect that the police must immediately be notified if the neighbor's wife -- everybody knows his neighbor very well -- has a fur coat remodelled or somebody is seen wearing a new ring or bracelet. We should like the Party to assist in this matter."

Correct?

Goering This is absolutely correct.

Jackson Now, Hilgard objected to your plan of releasing the insurance companies from paying the claims, did he not?

Goering Yes, this is also correct.

Jackson And he gave the reasons:

"Hilgard: If I may give the reasons for my objection, the point is that we do a large international business. Our business has a sound international basis, and in the interests of the foreign exchange position in Germany we cannot allow the confidence in the German insurance business to be shaken. If we were now to refuse to fulfil commitments entered into by legal contracts it would be a blot on the escutcheon of the German insurance business.

"Goering: But it would not be if I were to issue a decree or a law."

Am I quoting correct?

Goering Yes, and in Hilgard's reply -- and that is the reply I wanted to come to -- he pointed out that the insurance companies could not get out of paying claims unless a law provided for it. If the sovereign state passes a law to the effect that the insurance sums must be forfeited to the state, then the insurance companies are no longer under any obligation.

Jackson Now, I suggest to you that that is not correct, but that even though you proposed to issue a decree absolving the German insurance companies, the companies insisted on meeting their obligations; and then Heydrich interposed and said: "By all means, let them pay the claims and when payment is made it will be confiscated. Thus we will save our face."

Correct?

Goering Heydrich said that, but I issued a law.

Jackson Did you not then say:

"One moment. They will have to pay in any case because Germans suffered damage. There will, however, be a law forbidding them to make direct payments to Jews. They will also have to make payment for damage suffered by Jews, not to the Jews, but to the Minister of Finance.

"Hilgard: Aha."

Goering I have just said so.

Jackson You accepted Heydrich's suggestion, which was quite contrary to the one you made?

Goering No, I did not accept Heydrich's suggestion, but I issued a law to the effect that insurance money due to Jews must be paid to the Minister of Finance, as I did not agree with Heydrich that insurance money should be paid out and then surreptitiously confiscated. I went about it in a legal way and was not afraid to make the necessary law and to take the responsibility for the claims to be paid to the State, that is, to the Minister of Finance.

Jackson Well, the Tribunal will judge for itself, we have the evidence.

Now, Hilgard, representing the insurance companies, then raised the question that the amount of glass insurance premium was very important, that glass insurance was the companies' greatest asset, "but the amount of the damage now caused is twice as high as in an ordinary year," and he pointed out that the whole of the profits of the German insurance companies would be absorbed, did he not?

Goering Yes.

Jackson And also the question of the number of the stores destroyed -- Heydrich reported 7,500, is that right?

Goering Yes.

Jackson Now, I call your attention to the following conversation. Daluege...

Who, by the way, was he?

Goering Daluege was the leader of the Schutzpolizei.

Jackson "One question has still to be discussed. Most of the goods in the stores were not the property of the shopkeepers but were on consignment from other firms which had supplied them. Now the unpaid invoices are being sent in by these firms, which are certainly not all Jewish, but Aryan, in respect to these goods on consignment.

"Hilgard: We will have to pay for them too.

"Goering I wish you had killed 200 Jews instead of destroying such valuables.

"Heydrich: There were 35 killed."

Do I read that correctly?

Goering Yes, this was said in a moment of bad temper and excitement.

Jackson Spontaneously sincere, wasn't it?

Goering As I said, it was not meant seriously. It was the expression of spontaneous excitement caused by the events, and by the destruction of valuables, and by the difficulties which arose. Of course, if you are going to bring up every word I said in the course of 25 years in these circles, I myself could give you instances of even stronger remarks.

Jackson Then Funk interposed to discuss the foreign exchange point, did he not? He contributed to the discussion, did he not, for a while? I will not bother to go into it.

Goering Yes, but not everything is put down in the minutes, which are not clear on this point. I regret the minutes are incomplete. That is strange.

Jackson I join you in that. Hilgard returned again to the subject of the profit of the insurance companies, did he not?

Goering Yes, of course.

Jackson And you made this statement, did you not?

"The Jew must report the damage. He will get the insurance money, but it will be confiscated. The final result will be that the insurance companies will gain something, as not all damages will have to be made good. Hilgard, you can consider yourself damned lucky.

"Hilgard: I have no reason for that. The fact that we shall not have to pay for all the damage is called a profit.

"Goering: Just a moment. If you are legally bound to pay 5 millions and all of a sudden an angel, in my somewhat corpulent shape, appears before you and tells you, you may keep 1 million, hang it, is this not a profit? I should like to go 50-50 with you or whatever you call it. I only have to look at you, your whole body exudes satisfaction. You are getting a big rake-off."

Am I quoting correctly?

Goering Yes, of course, I said all that.

President We will break off now.

[The Tribunal recessed until 1400 hours.]

The Cross Examination of Goering
20th March 1946 - Afternoon

Jackson's questioning in the afternoon session touched on several areas. He first completed his listing of the harsh conditions imposed on Jews in Germany and Austria, and then moved onto a subject for which Goering became famous – his insatiable hunger for the artistic treasures of Europe.

Goering travelled through occupied countries and collected art from museums, galleries, churches and the so-called 'ownerless' Jewish art treasures, that is, art works that had been confiscated or extorted from Jews. He was not the principal collector of art for the Reich. That position was filled by the Special Staff Rosenberg (*Einsatzstab Rosenberg*) which had been tasked with the job of collecting artworks and transporting them to Germany. Goering acted independently, collecting artworks for himself and Hitler.

Of course, Goering's 'collecting' was simply stealing on a grand scale but there is a question over whether it would be permitted under the Geneva Conventions as part of an occupied country's contribution to the costs of occupation. Jackson did not deal with the question of legality, perhaps preferring to imply rather than prove the point. Considering the gravity of the crimes of which Goering had been accused, art theft was a minor matter.

Part way through Jackson's questioning over artworks, he had to face another embarrassment. He had been relying largely on material from Goering's interrogation by experts, and both Goering and his lawyer had been assured his answers would not be used against him. Jackson was not aware of this and had to stop this line of questioning immediately.

The questioning then touched on the employment of prisoners of war – mostly Russians – in the German economy. This may constitute a war crime as defined by the Geneva Conventions, if the prisoners are employed in the direct manufacturing of weapons and munitions. It is legal to employ prisoners in other fields, say agriculture or construction. It is also legal to employ them in the armaments industry as long as they are not directly concerned with weapons or munitions. Jackson did not investigate this but moved on to Goering's relations with the defendant Schacht and the mobilisation of German 15-year olds for the war effort.

Then Jackson faced another embarrassment. He brought up the subject of the bombing of Warsaw on 3rd September 1939 but instead of focussing on the possible bombing of civilian Polish targets, he concentrated only on the American ambassador's house which had been badly hit. He produced five aerial photographs of the damage and asked Goering if they had been taken by the Luftwaffe. Goering was quick to point out that they were oblique shots and so unlikely to be from the Luftwaffe which only took vertical shots. Also, there were no identifying marks on the backs of the photographs. Goering rubbed salt into Jackson's wounds by offering to comment on them anyway.

Then Jackson produced a piece of evidence that threw some light onto Goering's personal life. A proposal had been made to form commando units to operate in the forests behind enemy lines, disrupting military operations and creating confusion. Convicted game poachers were recommended as suitable recruits, but Goering had asked for this to be reconsidered. He was a lover of hunting and held the title of Hunting Master of the Reich (*Reichsjaegermeister*) and did not want dishonourable people doing a job that should have been done by proper hunters.

Testimony - Afternoon Session – 20th March 1946

Jackson I would like to call your attention again to the Exhibit USA-261, Document 1816-PS. Would you turn to Part 5, where you were speaking of Margraf's jewels that disappeared?

Goering That is going back to something already dealt with.

Jackson Yes, for a time, to Part 5. I call your attention to your statement as follows:

"Now we come to the damage sustained by the Jew, the disappearance of the jewels at Margraf's, *et cetera*. Well, they are gone and he will not get them refunded. He is the one who has to suffer the damage. Any of the jewels which may be returned by the police will belong to the State."

Do you find that?

Goering Yes, that is correct, but on the basis of the laws he was compensated for that.

Jackson Now, there was a representative of Austria present at this meeting, was there not?

Goering Yes.

Jackson And I ask you to turn to his statement in reference to conditions in Austria, a page or so farther on.

Goering Yes.

Jackson And I ask you whether he did not report to your meeting as follows:

"Your Excellency, in this matter, we have already a very complete plan for Austria. There are 12,000 Jewish workshops and 5,000 Jewish retail shops in Vienna. Even before the National Socialist revolution we already had, concerning these 17,000 shops, a definite plan for dealing with all tradesmen. Of the 12,000 workshops about 10,000 were to be closed definitely...."

Goering The interpreter did not follow ...

Jackson Do you find it?

Goering I have found it, but the interpreter has not.

Jackson "Regarding this total of 17,000 stores, of the shops of the 12,000 artisans, about 10,000 were to be closed definitely and 2,000 were to be kept open. Four thousand of the 5,000 retail stores were to be closed and 1,000 kept open, that is, were to be Aryanized. According to this plan, 3,000 to 3,500 of the total of 17,000 stores would be kept open, all others closed. This was decided following investigations in every single branch and according to local needs, in agreement with all competent authorities, and is ready for publication as soon as we shall receive the law which we requested in September. This law shall empower us to withdraw licenses from artisans quite independently of the Jewish question. That would be quite a short law.

"Goering: I shall have this decree issued today."

Goering Of course. This concerns a law for the curtailment of the heavy retail trade which, even apart from the Jewish question, would have reduced the number of retailers. That can be seen from the minutes.

Jackson Very well, let us go on a little further. Do you mean to inform the Tribunal that this did not apply to Jewish shops; that it had no connection with the Jewish question?

Goering I have said that independently of the Jewish question, in view of the overfilled retail trade, a limitation of the number of tradesmen would have followed, and that it can be seen from the following statement by Mr. Fischbock, which you have read, that I asked for a law which would authorize us to withdraw licenses, without any connection with the Jewish question. That would be a brief law. Whereupon I answered, "I will issue the decree today."

Jackson Now, if you will...

Goering Naturally, above all, Jewish stores were to be eliminated, as I said in the beginning.

Jackson Please go on down two paragraphs to where this was reported:

"But I do not believe that there will be 100 stores, probably fewer; and thus, by the end of the year, we would have liquidated all the recognized Jewish-owned businesses.

"Goering: That would be excellent.

"Fischbock:...."

Goering Yes, yes, that was the import of that meeting.

Jackson "Fischbock: Out, of 17,000 stores 12,000 or 14,000 would be shut down and the remainder Aryanized or handed over to the Trustee's office, which belongs to the State.

"Goering: I have to say that this proposal is grand. This way the whole affair in Vienna, one of the Jewish capitals so to speak, would be wound up by Christmas or by the end of the year.

"Funk: We can do the same thing here. I have prepared a law elaborating that. Effective 1 January 1939, Jews shall be prohibited from operating retail stores and wholesale establishments, as well as independent workshops. They shall be further prohibited from keeping employees, or offering any ready-made products on the market; from advertising or receiving orders. Whenever a Jewish shop is operated the police shall shut it down.

"From 1 January 1939 a Jew can no longer be head of an enterprise, as stipulated in the law for the organization of national labor of 20 January 1934. If a Jew has a leading position in an establishment without being the head of the enterprise, his contract may be declared void within 6 weeks by the head of the enterprise. With the expiration of this period all claims of the employee, including all claims to maintenance, become invalid. That is always very disagreeable and a great danger. A Jew cannot be a member of a corporation. Jewish members of corporations will have to be retired by 31 December 1938. A special authorization is unnecessary. The competent ministers of the

Reich are being authorized to issue the provision necessary for execution of this law.

"Goering: I believe we can agree with this law."

Goering Yes.

Jackson Now I ask you to pass a considerable dialogue relating to the Vienna situation, and I call your attention to the point at which Funk inquires of you:

"Why should the Jew not be allowed to keep bonds?"

"Goering: Because in that way he would actually be given a share."

Goering Yes, that was the purpose, to get him out of the enterprise. If he kept the bonds, on the basis of his rights as stockholder he still had an interest in the enterprise, and on the basis of ownership of stocks his will would still carry weight in the enterprise.

Jackson You turned Funk's suggestion down that the Jews be allowed to keep bonds?

Goering Yes. I replaced the bonds with securities.

Jackson Well, we will pass several more pages of debate, unless there is something you want to call attention to; and I come to the point where Heydrich is stating his position. I call your attention to this dialogue:

"Heydrich: At least 45,000 Jews were made to leave the country by legal measures.

"Goering:...."

Goering One moment, please. I find it now.

Jackson "At least 45,000 Jews were made to leave the country by legal measures.

"Goering: How was this possible?"

And then Heydrich tells you that: "... through the Jewish societies we extracted a certain amount of money from the rich Jews who wanted to emigrate. By paying this amount and an additional sum in foreign currency they made it possible for a number of poor Jews to leave. The problem was not to make the rich Jews leave but to get rid of the Jewish mob."

Is that correct?

Goering One moment. I do not find it here yet, but generally that is correct, yes.

Jackson Pass on a little further. Heydrich is making suggestions and says:

"As for the isolating, I would like to make a few proposals regarding police measures, which are important also because of their psychological effect on public opinion.

"For example, anybody who is Jewish according to the Nuremberg Laws will have to wear a certain badge. That is a possibility which will facilitate many other things. I see no danger of excesses, and it will make our relationship with the foreign Jews easier.

"Goering: A uniform?

"Heydrich: A badge. In this way we could put an end to foreign Jews being molested who do not look different from ours.

"Goering: But my dear Heydrich, you will not be able to avoid the creation of ghettos on a very large scale in all the cities. They will have to be created."

Is that what you said?

Goering I said that. At that time the problem was also to get the Jews together in certain parts of the cities and in certain streets, because on the basis of the tenancy regulations there was no other possibility, and if the wearing of badges was to be made obligatory, each individual Jew could have been protected.

Jackson Now, passing further in the discussion, I call your attention to this warning from Heydrich about the measures which have been discussed:

"Goering: Once we have a ghetto, we could determine what stores ought to be there and we would be able to say, 'You, Jew so and so, together with so and so, shall take care of the delivery of goods,' then a German wholesale firm will be ordered to deliver the goods for this Jewish store. The store would then not be a retail shop but a co-operative store, a co-operative society for Jews.

"Heydrich: All these measures will eventually lead to the institution of a ghetto. I must say: nowadays one should not want to set up a ghetto, but these measures, if carried through as outlined here, will automatically drive the Jews into a ghetto."

Did Heydrich give that warning?

Goering Here it says so, yes, but it can be seen from the following discussion that I said: "Now comes that which Goebbels mentioned before, compulsory renting. Now the Jewish tenants will come together." It was a question of the Jewish tenants drawing together, in order to avoid the disagreeable results which arose from reciprocal subletting.

Jackson You have omitted that Funk also remarked at this point that "Jews will have to stand together. What are 3 million? Everyone will have to stand up for the next fellow. Alone he will starve."

Do you find that?

Goering Yes. But in another part of these minutes it is stated very clearly: "One cannot let the Jews starve, and therefore the necessary measures must be taken."

Jackson Toward the close of that meeting you said the following, didn't you?

"I demand that German Jewry as a whole shall, as a punishment for the abominable crimes, *et cetera*, make a contribution of 1,000,000,000 marks. That will work. The pigs will not commit a second murder so quickly. Incidentally, I would like to say again that I would not like to be a Jew in Germany."

Goering That was correct, yes.

Jackson Were you joking about that too?

Goering I have told you exactly what led to the fine of 1,000,000,000.

Jackson You pointed out that the chauffeurs of Gauleiter must be prevented from enriching themselves through the Aryanization of Jewish property, right?

Goering Yes.

Jackson We will now take up the subject of art. I call your attention to Document 141-PS, Exhibit Number USA-308. That is the decree establishing priorities on the claim for Jewish art property. Do you recall that?

Goering That has been mentioned several times, and I have recently spoken about it in detail.

Jackson The order was issued as here stated, was it not?

Goering Yes, certainly; I emphasized that.

Jackson In Paragraph 5 reference is made to art objects that are suitable to be given to French museums, and which were to be sold by auction. The profit from this auction was to be given to the French State for the benefit of war widows and children. You say that this was never done?

Goering I did not say that this never happened. That was my intention in that decree.

Jackson Well, I am asking you if it ever has been done.

Goering As far as Paragraph 5 is concerned, I cannot say. I can only refer to the payments mentioned in Paragraph 2 -- the things that I pointed out -- which I had had effected after an estimate, and I said the other day that this amount was kept in readiness and that I repeatedly asked into which account it should be paid. And among the objects destined to go into the collection which I was to make, I had every single item valued.

Jackson Where was this amount kept?

Goering In my bank, under the name "Art Funds."

Jackson In what bank?

Goering It was -- I cannot say for sure, there were several banks -- in which bank exactly the art fund was deposited, I cannot say. I would have to have the documents here for that.

Jackson In the several interrogations you have never been able to point out where that fund is, have you?

Goering I cannot say, but you would only have to question my secretary who kept account of all the funds; she can tell you quite accurately.

Jackson This order, 141-PS, was carried out by the Rosenberg Special Staff (Einsatzstab), wasn't it?

Goering Yes.

Jackson Did you know who carried it out, who actually was there? Did you know Turner?

Goering I did not understand the name.

Jackson Did you know Mr. Turner?

Goering I know a certain Turner, who, however, had nothing to do with the Einsatzstab, the Rosenberg Special Staff and who, as far as I know, was in Yugoslavia.

Jackson Wasn't State Counsellor Turner in Paris in connection with the art collections?

Goering I repeat again so that no error is possible, you said Turner, T-u-r-n-e-r, or Korner, K-o-r-n-e-r?

Jackson Turner.

Goering Korner?

Jackson T-u-r-n-e-r.

Goering Turner -- I do not know whether he had anything to do with Rosenberg's Einsatzstab.

Jackson But you knew him, did you not?

Goering Yes.

Jackson And did you know a Dr. Bunjes?

Goering Bunjes, B-u-n-j-e-s, yes.

Jackson You knew him?

Goering Yes.

Jackson He had to do with captured or confiscated Jewish art treasures, did he not?

Goering I do not believe that Dr. Bunjes had anything to do with that. He was competent in a different field of art; but the Einsatzstab Rosenberg and certain departments of the military administration, had something to do with it.

Jackson I will ask to have you shown, so that you can follow me, to refresh your memory, Document 2523-PS, Exhibit Number USA-783, a letter from Dr. Bunjes, and ask you if this refreshes your recollection of certain events.

"On Tuesday, 4 February 1941, at 1830 hours I was ordered for the first time to report to the Reich Marshal at the Quai d'Orsay. Field Commander Von Behr of the Einsatzstab Rosenberg was present. It is, of course, difficult to describe in words the cordial atmosphere in which the conversation was held."

Do you recall such a meeting?

Goering No, it was not important enough for me to remember it, but I do not deny it, in any case.

Jackson We shall see if this refreshes your recollection:

"The Reich Marshal dropped the subject for the time being and asked for the report of the present state of the seizure of Jewish art property in the occupied western territories. On this occasion he gave Herr Von Behr the photographs of those objects of art that the Fuehrer wants to bring into his possession. In addition, he gave Herr Von Behr the photographs of those objects of art that the Reich Marshal wants to acquire for himself."

Goering I cannot follow here.

Jackson You mean you do not find these words, or you do not recall the events?

Goering No, I have not found the passage yet, and I would like to have a little time to see the context of this letter, which was neither written by me nor addressed to me.

Jackson Let me call your attention to a further paragraph of it and see if it does not refresh your recollection:

"On Wednesday, 5 February 1941, I was ordered to the Jeu de Paume by the Reich Marshal. At 1500 o'clock, the Reich Marshal, accompanied by General Hanesse, Herr Angerer, and Herr Hofer, visited the exhibition of Jewish art treasures newly set up there."

Goering Yes, I have already stated before that at Jeu de Paume I selected the art treasures which were exhibited there. That is right.

Jackson That is right; now we are getting there.

"Then, with me as his guide, the Reich Marshal inspected the exhibited art treasures and made a selection of those works of art which were to go to the Fuehrer, and those which were to be placed in his own collection.

"During this confidential conversation, I again called the Reich Marshal's attention to the fact that a note of protest had been received from the French Government against the activity of the Einsatzstab Rosenberg, with reference to the Hague Rules on Land Warfare recognized by Germany at the Armistice of Compiegne and I pointed out that General Von Stulpnagel's interpretation of the manner in which the confiscated Jewish art treasures are to be treated, was apparently contrary to the Reich Marshal's interpretation. Thereupon, the Reich Marshal asked for a detailed explanation and gave the following orders:

"First, it is my orders that you have to follow. You will act directly according to my orders. The art objects collected in the Jeu de Paume are to be loaded on a special train immediately and taken to Germany by order of the Reich Marshal. These art objects which are to go into the Fuehrer's possession, and those art objects which the Reich Marshal claims for himself, will be loaded on two railroad cars which will be attached to the Reich Marshal's special train, and upon his departure for Germany, at the beginning of next week, will be taken along to Berlin. FeldFuehrer Von Behr will accompany the Reich Marshal in his special train on the journey to Berlin.'

"When I made the objection that the jurists would probably be of a different opinion and that protests would most likely be made by the military commander in France, the Reich Marshal answered, saying verbatim as follows, 'Dear Bunjes, let me worry about that; I am the highest jurist in the State.'

"The Reich Marshal promised to send from his headquarters by courier to the Chief of the Military Administrative District of Paris on Thursday, 6 February, the written order for the transfer to Germany of the confiscated Jewish art treasures."

Now, does that refresh your memory?

Goering Not in the least, but it is not at all in contradiction to what I have said with respect to the art treasures, with the exception of one sentence. It is pure nonsense that I should have said that I was the highest jurist in the state because that, thank God, I was not. That is something which Mr. Bunjes said, and I cannot be held responsible for every statement which anyone may have made to somebody else without my having any possibility of correcting it. As for the rest, it corresponds to the statement I made recently.

Jackson Now, the art objects then were loaded on cars and shipped to Berlin, were they not?

Goering A part of them, yes.

Jackson I now call your attention to, and ask to have you shown, Document 014-PS, Exhibit Number USA-784.

Now, I ask you to refresh your recollection by following this report to the Fuehrer with me, and tell me if this conforms with your testimony:

"I report the arrival..."

Goering I would like to point out that this report did not come from me.

Jackson I understand that. I am asking if it is right or wrong.

"I report the arrival of the principal shipment of ownerless Jewish treasures of art at the salvage point Neuschwanstein by special train on Saturday the 15th of this month. It was secured by my Einsatzstab, in Paris. The special train, arranged for by Reich Marshal Hermann Goering, comprised 25 express baggage cars filled with the most valuable paintings, furniture, Gobelin tapestries, works of artistic craftmanship, and ornaments. The shipment consisted mainly of the most important parts of the collections of Rothschild, Seligmann" -- and half a dozen others.

Have you found that and is it correct?

Goering I do not know whether this is correct, since the report did not come from me. The only thing which I can remember is that I was asked by the Einsatzstab to see to it that a sufficient number of special cars, box cars was put at their disposal to ship the art treasures, since Jeu de Paume was not a safe place in case of air attacks. Neuschwanstein lies south of Munich. This concerns the objects destined for the Fuehrer.

I should like, however, to refer to the next sentence of this document, which was not written by me. It goes as follows:

"The confiscation actions of my Einsatzstab were begun in October 1940 in Paris according to your order, my Fuehrer."

That coincides with what I have said in my previous statements.

Jackson And would you care to read further?

Goering You mean where it says:

"Besides this special train, the main art objects selected by the Reich Marshal -- mainly from the Rothschild collection -- had previously been shipped in two special cars to Munich and were there put into the air raid shelter of the Fuehrerhaus."

They are those most precious works of art which I had designated for the Fuehrer, and which were to be sent, at the wish of the Fuehrer, to the air raid shelter. This had nothing to do directly with my affairs, but I did not dispute the fact, and I have explained it in detail.

Jackson When you were examined by the American Foreign Assets Commission, you estimated your art objects as having a value, at the time you turned them over to the government, of 50 million Reichsmark, as I recall it. Am I right?

Goering That is not quite correct. The Commission insisted on a valuation, and the discussion continued a long time backwards and forward. I expressly told the Commission that I could not assess the value because I did not have the objects in hand nor a list of them, and I could not quote them from memory; furthermore, that the estimates were subject to fluctuation depending on the one hand upon the prices art lovers might pay and, on the other, upon the actual market value. Since I did not see a copy of the minutes, in spite of my pleas, and especially as minutes of this nature often give rise to misunderstandings, I can only acknowledge the records which I have signed.

Jackson Well, do you question this fact? "When I gave the news to the Minister of Finance I estimated the value at that time at 50 million marks." Did you say that or did you not?

Goering I cannot estimate the value. I only told the Finance Minister that the entire collection, including my own, would be turned over to the State. And since I know my passion for collecting, I thought that it was quite possible that something might suddenly happen to me, and that as I had put my entire fortune into these works of art, the entire collection might possibly become State, that is, public property, and my family would thus be deprived of every means of subsistence. I therefore asked him to provide for a pension or some compensation for my family. That was the negotiation with the Finance Minister, to which he can testify.

Jackson What proportion of your art collection was acquired after 1933?

Goering I did not understand the question.

Jackson What proportion of your art collection was acquired after 1933?

Goering That I could not say in detail -- quite a number of pictures and statues.

Jackson Now, you have claimed that some part of your art collection you bought?

Goering Certainly.

Jackson And in connection with that some inquiry was made into your financial transactions, was there not?

Goering I do not know who made the inquiries.

Jackson Well, you were asked, were you not, about your receipt of 7,276,000 Reichsmark from the Reemtsma cigarette factory?

Goering No, I was never asked about that.

Jackson You were never asked about it?

Goering No, neither about the amount nor about the cigarette factory, nor anything else.

Jackson Let me refresh your recollection about that. Did you not tell them and did you not tell Colonel Amen in interrogations that this money was given to you by this cigarette factory and that their back taxes were cancelled?

Goering No, I even denied that their back taxes were ever cancelled. I remember now that the question was put to me in a different connection. A sum of money was set aside for the so-called Adolf Hitler Fund, and this amount the Fuehrer put at my disposal for general cultural tasks.

Jackson By the cigarette factory?

Goering Not by the cigarette factory; a number of business men subscribed to the Adolf Hitler Fund, and Mr. Reemtsma gave me this sum from the fund in the course of the years, after agreement with the Fuehrer. A part of it was allotted to the State theaters, another part for building up art collections, and other cultural expenditure.

Jackson Now, you were interrogated on the 22nd day of December 1945 by the External Assets Branch of the United States Investigation of Cartels and External Assets, were you not?

Goering May I first say explicitly that I had been asked whether I would be ready to make any statements about it, and was told that these statements would in no way be connected with this Trial. Therefore the presence of my defence counsel would not be necessary. This was expressly told me, and was repeated to me by the prison authorities, and before the interrogation it was again confirmed to me that these statements should in no way be brought in in connection with this Trial. However, that is all the same to me. You may produce them as far as I am concerned. But because of the method employed, I desire to have this made known here.

Dr Stahmer I protest against the use of the statements for the reason that has just been given by the witness. I myself sometime ago -- I think it was around Christmas -- was asked by, I believe, members of the United States Treasury whether they could interrogate the Defendant Goering on questions of property, adding expressly that I did not have to be present at the interrogation because this had nothing to do with the Trial, and would not be used for it.

Jackson I am not able either to affirm or deny, and therefore I will not pursue this subject further at this time. I do not believe that any stipulation was made that these facts should not be gone into. I was not informed of it, and if there has been, of course, it would be absurd.

[Turning to the witness.] Now, you were asked about receiving some art objects from Monte Cassino.

Goering Yes.

Jackson I ask you if it is not the fact that an altar statue taken from the Cassino Abbey was brought and delivered to you, and that you expressed great appreciation for it.

Goering I am glad to be able to clarify this affair also. After the monastery of Monte Cassino had been completely destroyed by shelling and had been defended by a paratroop division, a delegation arrived one day bringing along a statue of some saint, entirely worthless from an artistic point of view, as a souvenir of this destroyed monastery. I thanked the men and showed the statue to the curator of my art collection, and he also considered the statue as of absolutely no value. It then remained in the box and was put away somewhere. The other ...

President I do not think this is coming through sufficiently loud for the shorthand writers to hear.

Goering The rest of the art treasures from Monte Cassino, according to my knowledge, were shipped in the following manner: A large part, especially those objects which belonged to the old monastery itself, was sent to the Vatican. I must assume this from the fact that the abbot of the monastery sent me and my division a letter written in Latin in which he expressed his extreme gratitude for this action.

Secondly, as far as I remember, the art treasures from the museum in Naples, which were at Monte Cassino, were for the greater part sent by us to Venice and there turned over to the Italian Government. Some pictures and statues were brought to Berlin, and there they were turned over to me. On the very same day I gave the list to the Fuehrer, and some time later also the objects themselves which were in my air raid shelter, so that he could negotiate about the matter with Mussolini. I did not keep a single one of these objects for my own collection. If my troops had not intervened, these priceless art treasures, which were stored in Monte Cassino and belonged to the monastery there, would have been entirely destroyed by enemy bombardment, that is to say, by the British-American attackers. Thus they have been saved.

Jackson Now, you say of no value -- no substantial value?

Goering That is even now my conviction, and I depended, above all, on the judgment of my experts. I never took this statue out of its packing case. It did not interest me. On the other hand, I wanted to say a few words of thanks to the men who brought it.

Jackson The labor shortage in the Reich was becoming acute by November of 1941, was it not?

Goering That is correct.

Jackson And you yourself gave the directives for the employment of Russian prisoners of war, did you not?

Goering Employment for what?

Jackson For war industry -- tanks, artillery pieces, airplane parts.

Goering That is correct.

Jackson That was at the conference of the 7th of November 1941, that you gave that order, was it not?

Goering At what conference that was I could not tell you; I issued these directives only in a general way.

Jackson And the directive was that Russian prisoners of war should be selected in collecting camps beyond the Reich border, and should be transported as rapidly as possible and employed in the following order of priority: mining, railroad maintenance, war industry -- tanks, artillery pieces, airplane parts, agriculture, building industry, *et cetera*. You gave that order, did you not?

Goering If I have signed it, the order is from me. I do not remember details.

President What was the number of that, Mr. Jackson?

Jackson I ask to have you shown Document Number 1193-PS.

Goering I have not seen it yet.

[Document 1193-PS was submitted to the witness.]

This document, which you have just mentioned ...

Jackson I did not get the answer.

Goering Excuse me. I have just received a document about the use of Russian troops. Is that the document of which you speak?

Jackson That is right. I call your attention to the fact that it is referred to as an annex in the letter signed by Goering.

Goering I want to point out that this document is not signed by me, but by Korner, which, however, does not diminish my responsibility.

Jackson Well, you do not question that on the 7th day of November 1941, you gave the order, as Korner reports it, do you, in the document referred to as 1193-PS?

Goering I said only that it was not signed by me but by Korner, and here even a still younger official, a Regierungsrat, and I wanted only to explain that this was my field and that therefore I assume responsibility. But I have not read it through yet. This deals with directives and outlines which I gave in general and which were then filled in and revised by the department concerned, whereby naturally not every word or every sentence written here was said or dictated by myself. But that does not alter the fact that I bear the responsibility for it, even if I did not know it in detail, or would have perhaps formulated it differently. But the general directives were given by me and implemented accordingly by the lesser authorities.

Jackson You also gave the order, did you not, that 100,000 men were to be taken from among the French prisoners of war not yet employed in armament industry? Gaps in manpower resulting therefrom will be filled by Soviet prisoners of war. The transfer of the above-named French prisoners of war is to be accomplished by October the 1st. You gave the order, did you not?

Goering That is correct. Here we deal primarily with the fact that a large part of French skilled workers who were prisoners of war were turned into free workers on condition that they worked in the German armament industry. The shortages which occurred at their previous places of work at that time, where they had worked as prisoners of war, were to be remedied by Russian prisoners of war, because I considered it pointless that qualified skilled industrial workers should be employed in agriculture, for instance, or in any other field not corresponding to their abilities. Thus there was an incentive in the fact that these people could become free workers instead of remaining prisoners of war, if they would agree to these conditions. The directives were given by me.

Jackson And did you know that there was any forced labor employed in Germany?

Goering Compulsory labor.

Jackson Did you not testify under interrogation on the 3rd of October 1945, that:

"I would like to add something to the last question of the interrogation. The Colonel asked me if the forced labor program was effective, and I said 'Yes'. There are two remarks I would like to make to that.

"All right.

"I must say that in the results as such it was effective. However, a great number of acts of sabotage did occur, and also treason and espionage.

"Question: But on the whole you would say it was a successful program from the German point of view?

"Answer: Yes. Without this manpower many things could never have been achieved."

Did you say that?

Goering That is obvious, because without workers one cannot do any work.

President I do not think you answered the question. The question was if you said the forced labor had been a success. What do you have to say to that? Did you say that?

Goering I have said what I did in answering the question whether the manpower used was successful; yes, that is correct.

Jackson Now, you were shown a document, 3700-PS, written by Schacht to you, and you have said that you received it?

Goering Yes, I remember.

Jackson Now, you and Schacht were somewhat rivals in the economic field at one period, were you not?

Goering I explained that only recently, and to what extent.

Jackson You wanted his position abolished in the event of war and he wanted your position abolished in event of war, did he not -- your economic position?

Goering Not quite. They were two similar authorities having similar powers at the same time, two personalities, and that in the long run was not possible. It simply had to be decided which one of the two should be the sole authority. That would have been especially necessary in case of a mobilization.

Jackson You, in testifying on the 17th day of October last, as to your relations with Schacht, made this statement, did you not, in reference to your disagreements with Schacht: "This I must underline: Schacht always tried to manoeuvre for a new post, while all the other ministers co-operated absolutely." Did you say that?

Goering Not exactly as it is there, but I wanted to emphasize that, contrary to the other ministers who obediently followed my directives for the Four Year Plan, I had certain difficulties with Schacht, which I have already explained, due to his original and strong personality.

Jackson The question was whether you made that statement in substance or in those words?

Goering Not exactly in these words, but as I have just explained, in substance.

Jackson Now, do you have in mind Schacht's letter to you, Document Number 3700-PS?

Goering Yes, I read it a short time ago.

Jackson And in that letter Schacht said this to you, did he not, referring to 3700-PS? "   It may be militarily necessary. . . "Do you want to follow it?

[Document 3700-PS was submitted to the witness.]

"It may be militarily necessary to conscript the 15-year-olds, but it will heavily tax the fighting morale of the German people. The facts as the German people see them are as follows:

"First, the original prospect of a short war has not been realized.

"Second, the prospective quick victory over England by the Air Force did not materialize.

"Third, the public statement that Germany would remain free of enemy air raids has not been fulfilled.

"Fourth, the repeated announcements that the Russian resistance was definitely broken have been proved to be untrue.

"Fifth, Allied supplies of arms to Russia, and the manpower reserves of Russia have, on the contrary, been sufficient to bring continuous heavy counterattacks against our Eastern Front.

"Sixth, the original victorious advance into Egypt has been halted after repeated attempts.

"Seventh, the landing of the Allies in North and West Africa, declared impossible, has nevertheless been accomplished.

"Eighth, the extremely large amount of shipping space which was required for this landing has shown that our U-boats, in spite of their great successes, did not suffice to prevent this transport. In addition, the reductions in civilian traffic, in material for armaments, and in the availability of manpower are obvious to all the people.

The conscription of the 15-year-olds will increase the doubts concerning the termination of this war."

Can you fix any more definitely than you have done the date when you received that letter?

Goering I can only say again that it is dated the 3rd of November, but the year is missing. If I were to be given a copy where the year is stated, I could give an exact answer. I have said recently that, according to my knowledge of events, it is a question of either November 1944 or November 1943. But, unfortunately, that is not indicated here. I can only see 3rd of November. The year is missing.

Jackson Do you know when Schacht was sent to the concentration camp? Do you know the date of that?

Goering Not exactly, but now that you remind me of it, I can say that this letter certainly was not written in 1944 because in November 1944, I believe, Mr. Schacht was already in the concentration camp; consequently, it must date back to November 1943.

Jackson And he was sent to the concentration camp shortly after dispatching that letter to you, wasn't he?

Goering No, that is not correct.

Jackson How much longer was he at large?

Goering The letter is of 3 November 1943, as we have just found. I heard about the arrest of Schacht only after the attempt on the life of the Fuehrer and after my return a few days later, after an illness of some time, that is to say, in September 1944. There is not the least connection between this letter and his arrest, because, when I asked about his arrest, I was told definitely it was in connection with the 20th of July.

Jackson Did you make an agreement, as Supreme Commander of the Air Force, with the ReichsFuehrer SS, the Youth Fuehrer of the German Reich, and the Reich Minister for Occupied Eastern Territories, about the recruiting of youthful Russians, Ukrainians, White Russians, Lithuanians, and Tartars between the ages of 15 and 20? Did you come to some agreement with Himmler and Rosenberg about that?

Goering That I personally concluded such an agreement, I do not think so. It is possible and even probable that my office did so, however.

Jackson And you have testified yesterday or the day before -- I think Friday -- as follows; let me refresh your recollection about the questions of confiscations.

"Now, about the question of confiscation of State property and it was only such property that was confiscated. As far as I know, private property is mentioned in the official report as far as the winter of 1941 and 1942 is concerned, that might have been the case in the matter of furs or perhaps fur boots, and some soldiers may have taken little odds and ends from the people; but on the whole there was no private property and so none could be confiscated."

And I think you also said that you never took anything, not even so much as a screw or a bolt, when you were in occupation of foreign territory. Do you recall that testimony?

Goering Very exactly.

Jackson Do you still stand on it?

Goering Of course.

Jackson I ask to have you shown a Document EC-317.

Goering Yes.

Jackson Now, that is a secret command matter, is it not, dated the 7th of September 1943? Is that right?

Goering I have a letter here before me of 21 February 1944.

Jackson Then you have the wrong exhibit -- EC-317, Page 3.

Goering Yes; Page 3.

Jackson This letter of transmittal we will not bother about. Your secret command matter is dated 7 September 1943, is it not?

Goering That is correct.

Jackson And it reads as follows:

"Concerning the removal of the harvested crops and the destruction of the means of production in the agricultural and food economy in parts of the Occupied Eastern Territories.

"By direction of the Fuehrer, I give the following orders:

"First: In the territories east of the line fixed by the highest military command, the following measures are to be taken gradually, according to the military situation at the time. The measures are to be determined by the commanders of the army groups:

"(1) All agricultural products, means of production, and machinery of enterprises serving the agriculture and food industry are to be removed.

" (2) The factories serving the food economy, both in the field of production and of processing, are to be destroyed.

"(3) The basis of agricultural production, especially the records and establishments, storage plants, *et cetera*, of the organizations responsible for the food economy, are to be destroyed.

"(4) The population engaged in the agricultural and food economy is to be transported into the territory west of the fixed line."

Right?

Goering Absolutely correct; but I want to make the following statement in connection with it. We are dealing here with purely military measures in a retreat, and may I comment on these four points: I emphasized the other day that a great number of agricultural machines had been brought to Russia by us. As the Russians, in their retreat, destroyed everything, we had all the less military reason to allow the machinery of industries which we had set up and brought there to fall into their hands undestroyed. This concerns an urgently necessary military order which had been issued during a retreat, and which was executed in the same way as before in the reverse sense. It does not deal with any sort of private property.

Jackson And it was signed by you?

Goering Yes, this order bears my signature.

Jackson I am about to go into a different subject, may it please Your Honor.

President Yes, we will adjourn now.

[A recess was taken.]

Jackson I will ask that the witness be shown a document, 3786-PS, of which there are no extra copies available because it came to us so late. I will ask you to examine that and tell me whether you recall the meeting to which these minutes refer?

Goering We are apparently concerned here with a report dealing with a meeting which took place daily with the Fuehrer. As meetings occurred once or twice daily, I naturally cannot, with any accuracy, without first having read the report, recall the report of 27 January 1945, for I was present at a great number of these meetings during the course of the war.

Jackson I shall call your attention to specific incidents in it. The minutes indicate that the Fuehrer, yourself, Keitel, and Jodl were present, were they not?

Goering That is according to the notes.

Jackson And I will call your attention to Page 31 and ask you to follow with me the notes and see if it refreshes your recollection. Now this relates to 10,000 imprisoned air force officers. I quote what is attributed to you.

"Goering: Near Sagan, there are 10,000 imprisoned air force officers. Their custody is the responsibility of the Commander-in-Chief of the Reserve Army (B.d.E.). Personnel for guarding or transporting them is said to be lacking. The suggestion was made as to whether the prisoners should not be left to their Soviet Russian allies. It would give them 10,000 airmen.

"The Fuehrer: Why did you not remove them earlier? This is an unequalled bungling.

"Goering: That is the business of the commander of the B.d.E. We have nothing to do with it. I can only report it.

"The Fuehrer: They must be removed, even if they have to go on foot. The Volkssturm must be called in. Anyone who escapes will be shot. Any means must be used.

"Goering: That is from Sagan, there are 10,000 men.

"Guderian: In the transfer process the 4th Armored Division has been moved out completely, also the 227th Division; the remainder of the 32d Division is now moving out. The next in line is the Headquarters of the 3rd SS Panzer Corps which will move tonight, and tomorrow night the Division Niederland, which has already pulled out. Parts of the Division Nordland have also been withdrawn from the front.

"The Fuehrer: Are they to get replacements? Are they already on the move?

"Guderian: Fegelein took care of that. He has already ordered that they should be replenished immediately.

"The Fuehrer: It is absolutely clear that the Army Group Vistula has nothing, for the time being, besides the Corps Nehring, the one group, and what it has on the Vistula. This must be organized. It will come from here and partly from Germany. It must be done, notwithstanding.

"Goering: How many cattle cars are needed for 10,000 men?

"The Fuehrer: If we transport them according to German standards, then we need at least 20 transport trains for 10,000 men. If we transport them according to Russian standards, we need 5 or 3.

"Goering: Take their pants and boots off so that they cannot walk in the snow."

Do you recall that incident?

Goering I remember this incident but vaguely.

Now that I have given the answer I would like to give a short explanation of the value of this document. I understood that this document has just now arrived, but I have already been interrogated with respect to this document long before the beginning of the proceedings. Already at that time I pointed out that at the stenographic recording of a meeting two stenographers took notes at the same time, since the meetings often lasted 4 or 5 hours, and therefore these stenographic notes always had to be gone over afterwards, especially as frequently, because of the presence of many men, inaccuracies occurred in the recordings so that statements made by one person were credited to another in the minutes. For that reason I said at that time already that not only did I not remember this statement, but that in my opinion I have never made this statement. We were concerned solely with the preparation of motor vehicles for transport.

Jackson Well, I must say that you were interrogated with reference to the incident, but not with reference to these notes which were not transcribed.

Goering In respect to this transcript and this incident, it was especially emphasized that we were concerned with the stenotype record of the report of the meeting, and I already uttered a similar opinion at that time. It was not submitted to me at that time.

Jackson Not stenotype, but stenographic.

You are also reported on Page 35. 1 call your attention to this and ask you, is it attributed to you mistakenly?

"Goering: The 10,000 prisoners in Sagan should be transported away by ObergruppenFuehrer Rittner." Perhaps I do not pronounce the word as you would.

"The Fuehrer: These prisoners must be removed by all available means. Volkssturm must be employed with the most energetic men. All who attempt to flee will be shot."

"Fegelein: We have a man for that who guards the concentration camps. That is GruppenFuehrer Glucks. He must do the job."

Did that occur?

Goering That I do not know. I have already testified before that the B.d.E. had to take charge of the transportation, because we had nothing to do with it. What ideas and opinions the other gentlemen expressed in the discussions I cannot completely testify to, or state here. It was a question of whether these 10,000 were to be surrendered or shipped away.

Jackson I will ask you a question or two about the Warsaw bombing. Was it known to you that on the 3rd of September, the house of the Ambassador of the United States, situated some 17 kilometers out of Warsaw, was bombed by the German Air Force?

Goering No; that is unknown to me.

Jackson Your Air Force took a good many pictures of the Polish villages and of Warsaw and used them for distributing among the German people, didn't they?

Goering That is possible, I was not concerned with that. In any event, the Luftwaffe did not distribute pictures to the German people. It is possible that pictures taken by the Luftwaffe might have got into the German press by way of the Propaganda Ministry. But distribution, in the sense of the Luftwaffe's distributing photographs like leaflets, never occurred.

Jackson The Luftwaffe did take the pictures for the purpose of determining the efficiency of its hits, did it not?

Goering The Luftwaffe took pictures before the target was bombed, and again after the target had been bombed, to determine whether the target had actually been hit.

Jackson I ask to have you shown five photographs and ask you if those are not photographs taken by the Luftwaffe, following the attack on Poland.

[Photographs were shown to the witness.]

Goering To answer the first question, whether the pictures had actually been taken by the German Air Force, I regret I cannot give a positive answer for there is no indication that these were made by the German Air Force. Four out of the five pictures were, if you observe them closely, taken from an oblique angle, as though they had been taken from a church steeple rather than from an airplane, from which generally only vertical pictures are taken because of the built-in camera.

The picture showing the destruction of parts of Warsaw can be regarded technically as such an aerial photo. The date is lacking here. But none of these pictures give any proof that they were taken by the Luftwaffe.

However, let us assume that they were taken by the Luftwaffe, so that further questions will be facilitated.

Jackson You say you will assume they were by the Luftwaffe?

Goering Yes, although I doubt it.

Jackson I do not want you to give away anything here. If you think they were not taken by the Luftwaffe, I do not want you to admit it.

Goering I said there is no proof. I did not take the pictures, I do not recognize them, they were not submitted to me as Luftwaffe pictures and from a purely technical point of view they could only have been taken from a plane with a private camera from a very oblique angle. They are not true aerial pictures, that is vertical pictures as taken by the Air Force.

Jackson Well, we will pass them then and go to something else.

Let us take up Document 638-PS, Exhibit Number USA-788, about which you have been interrogated and which, as I recall, you authenticated.

[Document 638-PS was submitted to the witness.]

This is the document which was signed by Dr. Joel and I ask you to follow me.

"From the Reich Marshal's plans of 24 September 1942.

"First: The Reich Marshal is looking for daring fellows who will be employed in the East as Sonderkommandos and who will be able to carry out the task of creating confusion behind the lines. They are to be formed into bands under leadership, and with interpreters assigned to them. For this purpose the Reich Marshal is considering convicts who are first offenders, who have committed not particularly heinous offenses for which there can be some human understanding.

"The Reich Marshal first of all mentioned persons convicted of poaching. He knew, of course, that the ReichsFuehrer SS had picked out the so-called poachers, and they were already in his hands. He requests, however, that the question be re-examined. The only suitable men are those with a passion for hunting, who have poached for love of the trophy, not men who have laid snares and traps. The Reich Marshal also mentioned fanatical members of smuggling gangs, who take part in gun battles on the frontiers and whose passion it is to outwit the customs at the risk of their own lives, but not men who attempt to bring articles over the frontier in an express train or by similar means.

"The Reich Marshal leaves it to us to consider whether still another category of convicts can be assigned to these bands or pursuit commands.

"In the regions assigned for their operations, these bands, whose first task should be to destroy the communications of the partisan groups, could murder, burn and ravish; in Germany they would once again come under strict supervision.

"Signed: Dr. Joel, 24 September 1942."

Do you wish to make an explanation of that document to the Tribunal?

Goering Yes, with the same that I made once before. The first two paragraphs clearly show that I wanted only those people who had committed no offenses involving laws of honor, such as poachers, distinguishing between those having a passion for hunting and those who only want to steal. I made a distinction also with regard to smugglers, between those who take personal risks showing a certain passion for their activity, and those who do it in a dishonorable way.

Both these main paragraphs plainly show that I did not wish to use criminals of any type, and that is why I explicitly denied having said what is stated in the last paragraphs. It is not a question of the minutes but of the notes taken by an official with whom I discussed these things. He should be able to testify where and if he heard these words uttered by me. But they contradict my ideas so much, and I particularly emphasize this, and in particular, as I have clearly said, as regards rape, which I always punished with death even if committed against citizens of enemy states, that I rejected that statement; and I again pointed out that the main paragraphs are in utmost contradiction to the last remark, because if it had been a matter of indifference to me, I could have selected criminals.

Thirdly, I expressly stated above, that their main task behind the lines was to create confusion, to disrupt communications, to destroy railways, and the like. Fourthly and lastly, the whole thing never took place.

Jackson You objected to the word "ravish" which had been translated the first time "rape", and that is the only objection you made to this document when it was presented to you. Is that not correct?

Goering No, it is not correct that way. I say this because it is a most significant concept which has always particularly contradicted my sense of justice, for shortly after the seizure of power I instigated a sharpening of this phase of German penal laws. And I wanted to show by this word and this concept, that this entire latter part could not have been uttered by me, and I deny having said it. I will absolutely and gladly take responsibility for even the most serious things which I have done, but I deny this statement, as being in complete contradiction to my opinions.

Jackson Who is the signer of this document?

Goering Dr. Joel.

Jackson Yes -- you knew him?

Goering I knew him slightly. I saw him at this conference.

Jackson He was present at the conference?

Goering I instructed him to come to tell him that I wished that type of people.

Jackson Now, you dealt in economic matters with the various occupied countries through Reichskommissars?

Goering I testified the other day that all sorts of authorities, including the Reichskommissars had to follow my economic directives and orders.

Jackson And were to report to you on economic matters?

Goering Not about all of them, only insofar as they concerned my directives.

Jackson And who was your Reichskommissar in Poland?

Goering There was no Reichskommissar, in Poland. There was a Governor General in Poland, that was Dr. Frank.

Jackson And who was the Reichskommissar in the Netherlands?

Goering Dr. Seyss-Inquart was Reichskommissar for Holland.

Jackson Who was the Reichskommissar for Norway?

Goering In Norway the Gauleiter Terboven was Reichskommissar.

Jackson Terboven -- he was also a Gauleiter you say?

Goering He was Gauleiter at Essen.

Jackson You appointed him to Norway or attained his appointment?

Goering I neither appointed him for Norway -- because that was beyond my jurisdiction -- nor did I have him appointed. I did not oppose his appointment in any way as I considered he would make a very competent Reichskommissar.

Jackson And he was there from 1940 until 1945?

Goering I believe that is correct.

Jackson Now, I will ask to have you shown Document R-134, a communication from Terboven to you.

[Document R-134 was submitted to the witness.]

That is a communication of the 1st of May 1942, is it not?

Goering I note the date; yes.

Jackson And that reports to you as follows, does it not -- it is addressed to you as Reich Marshal, "My esteemed Reich Marshal", is that right?

Goering Yes.

Jackson Omitting the first paragraph, unless you are to give it.

"Several days ago on an island west of Bergen we captured a Norwegian sabotage unit, trained by the Secret Service, and found extensive stores of sabotage instruments, some of them of a new kind, including probably poison and bacteria. Those which appeared unfamiliar were forwarded to the Reich Security Main Office for closer examination.

"Besides other tasks, this sabotage unit was to begin its sabotage work, on Sola and Herdla using the explosive of which a sample is enclosed herewith. This appears from written directives found. Since it must be assumed that similar actions are under way on airfields on the rest of the European coast, and assuming that a means of sabotage actually unknown until now is involved, I am communicating with you by the fastest possible means, in order to give you an opportunity to issue an appropriate warning.

"Unfortunately, two especially reliable officers of the Security Police were killed in the fight against the sabotage unit. We buried them this morning at 1000 hours in the Heroes' Cemetery in Bergen.

"On the same day and at the same hour 18 Norwegians were shot on my order. These had been captured some time previously in the attempt to go to England illegally.

"On the same day, the entire village which had harbored the

sabotage unit was burned down and the population deported. All the males were taken to a German concentration camp without any notification being sent to their families. The women were sent to a female forced labor camp in Norway, and those children who were not capable of working went to a children's camp. Heil Hitler! Yours obediently, Terboven."

Is that correct?

Goering It says so in the letter, a copy of which is before me.

Jackson Terboven remained after that report until 1945, didn't he?

Goering That's correct.

Jackson Now, later in the same year, 1942, you adopted very similar means to those reported by Terboven to you, did you not?

Goering I did not understand the question.

Jackson Well you adopted later in the same year the same means as Terboven, didn't you?

Goering I? Where?

Jackson Well, I will ask that you be shown Document 1742-PS.

[Document 1742-PS was submitted to the witness.]

Now, this is a decree of 26 October 1942, by Goering. I ask you to follow me:

"Simultaneously with the intensified combating of guerrilla activity ordered by the Fuehrer, and the cleaning up of the land behind the lines, in particular that behind the Army Group Center, I request that the following points be taken into consideration, and the conclusions drawn therefrom be put into practice:

"Simultaneously with the combating of the underground forces and the combing out of the areas contaminated by them, all available livestock must be driven off to safe areas. Similarly, food supplies are to be removed and brought into safety, so that they will no longer be available to the guerrillas.

"2. All male and female labor suitable for any kind of employment must be forcibly recruited and allocated to the Plenipotentiary General for Labor, who will then employ them in safe areas behind the lines or in the Reich. Separate camps must be organized behind the lines for the children."

Is that right?

Goering Absolutely. It concerns areas overrun by guerrillas, and no one could expect me to leave cattle and foodstuffs at their disposal. Furthermore, people who were repeatedly being incited to guerrilla activities and revolts against us had to be brought back to safe areas and put to work. I would like to emphasize that this was absolutely vital for the security of the troops. But I may emphasize again that you said I gave the same orders which you read from Terboven's letter. I did not order villages to be burned, and did not order the shooting of hostages. This was something basically different.

Jackson You simply seized all the men, women and children and moved them out. That is what I referred to.

By May of 1944 your problem in the loss of fighter aircraft and fighter personnel was becoming serious?

Goering Yes.

Jackson On the 19th of May, 1944, you had a conference in your office, on the subject of fighter aircraft and the losses of fighter personnel, did you not?

Goering Yes.

Jackson And you have been shown the minutes of that meeting and authenticated them in your interrogations?

Goering It is not the minutes of that conference. It is a short and brief summary by an officer of a meeting which, as far as I know, lasted 2 days.

Jackson I will ask to have you shown Document L-166. It is entitled, "Most Secret Document," isn't it?

Goering That is correct.

Jackson And it is also entitled, "Minutes of conference on fighter aircraft with the Reich Marshal on 15 and 16 May 1944." That is correct, too, is it not?

Goering No, it says, "Notices of a conference on fighter aircraft at the Reich Marshal's on 15 and 16 May 1944."

Jackson "Notices," you translate it "notices"?

Goering It says "memorandum" here and that is the original.

Jackson "Notes of Conference on Fighter Aircraft."

Goering Lasting 2 days.

Jackson Yes. And at first General Galland described in detail the situation regarding fighter personnel. That took place, didn't it, and he reviewed the losses?

Goering Yes.

Jackson And reviewed the losses?

Goering That is right.

Jackson And then he reviewed at some length under Item 2, "Remedial Measures," is that right?

Goering According to the memorandum, yes, but whether that actually took place I cannot say.

Jackson This conference took place, didn't it?

Goering Absolutely, 2 days.

Jackson And under Item 3 General Galland made certain proposals, did he not?

Goering Yes.

Jackson And then after considerable discussion General Schmidt made certain proposals, Items 12 and 13, is that right?

Goering It must have been so. At any rate it says so according to the memorandum.

Jackson You recommended a conference between the chief of the General Staff and the chief of artillery, as soon as possible, did you not? Item 13?

Goering Yes.

Jackson And General Schmidt's recommendations and requests appear in Items 14 and 15 and 16 and 17 and 18?

Goering Yes.

Jackson Then you decided:

"The Reich Marshal has decided that only the III-groups of fighter squadrons are to remain in the Reich, and that all the fighters fit for operations are to be pressed into service."

That occurred, did it not?

Goering Yes.

Jackson Then:

"The Reich Marshal desires that when low-level attack on airfields are made, causing considerable loss in personnel and material, the measures taken for defence and dispersal are to be re-examined by the Luftwaffenfuhrungsstab."

Number 19. That occurred, did it not?

Goering Yes.

Jackson Item 20 reads:

"The Reich Marshal wishes to propose to the Fuehrer that American and English crews who shoot indiscriminately over towns, at moving civilian trains, or at soldiers hanging to parachutes should be shot immediately on the spot."

Have I correctly read that?

Goering It says so here. And I objected at once at that time that this was not correct. This passage has no connection at all with the context of these notes, 19-21. Besides the expression "soldiers hanging to parachutes" is entirely misleading and not commonly used. I thought for a long time about how this could have got into the notes, which I never saw and which were drawn up over a period of 2 days, and can only find the explanation that I pointed out -- as can be gathered from the other evidence -- that around that time the Fuehrer gave a directive in that connection, and that in any event there must be a mistake; that is, it should not be that the Reich Marshal wants to propose, *et cetera*, to the Fuehrer, but that I might have suggested that the Fuehrer had some such intention. But about this the author of these notes would have to be consulted. No other item in all these notes refers to this. Even the next item is entirely different. Whereas everything else stands in relationship, this one point is extraneous.

Jackson In all the notes of the 2 days, this is the one thing that you say is mistaken.

Now I ask to have you shown Document 731-PS.

[Document 731-PS was submitted to the witness.]

Now, the conference, the notes of which I have just read you, was followed within a week by the order, 731-PS, was it not, the memorandum, 731-PS, which reads:

"The Fuehrer has reached the following decision in regard to measures to be taken against Anglo-American air crews in special instances:

"Enemy airmen who have been brought down are to be shot without court martial proceedings in the following instances..."

President Mr. Justice Jackson, shouldn't you refer to a passage four lines above that, after "Report of the Reich Marshal"?

Jackson I did not, but perhaps for the record it ought to be in full.

"Chief of the Command Staff of the Armed Forces, Chief WFSt. Please direct drafting of order. W (Warlimont). K (Keitel), Deputy Chief of Command Staff of the Armed Forces. Must go to ReichsFuehrer SS. According to the report of the Reich Marshal, General Korten made the following statement: 'Memorandum' " -- I think the next line is not in the original --

"The Fuehrer has given the following ruling in regard to measures to be taken against Anglo-American air crews in special instances:

"Enemy airmen whose machines have been shot down are to be

shot without trial by court martial in the following cases:

"(1) In the event of the shooting of our own German air crews while they are parachuting to earth.

"(2) In the event of aerial attacks upon German planes which have made emergency landings and whose crews are in the immediate vicinity.

"(3) In the event of attacks upon railway trains engaged in public transport.

"(4) In the event of low-level aerial attacks upon individual civilians, farmers, workers, single vehicles, and so forth.'"

Now, there is a note: "In the event of low-level aerial attacks on individual civilians, single civilian vehicles, and so forth," is there not?

Goering On my copy, "In the event of low-level aerial attacks on single" -- "single" is crossed out here and there are two words written above which I cannot read. Before the expression, "single vehicles," is the word "civilian" and referring to Point 2, it says:

"I consider it doubtful, because the destruction of a plane which has made an emergency landing cannot be designated as gangster methods but rather as a measure in keeping with the strictest standards of civilized warfare."

We are concerned with the entire series of questions discussed in these days and weeks and to which Von Brauchitsch also testified recently.

Jackson That note about that emergency landing is signed by "J", isn't it, which, stands for "Jodl"?

Goering Certainly.

Jackson I think that is all I care to ask.

There are a number of documents which should be introduced in this connection, and I think it will be best perhaps if we tabulate them and get them ready over the evening and present them in the morning.

President Certainly, Mr. Justice Jackson, you can put them all in then.

The Cross Examination of Goering
20th March 1946 – Afternoon (continued) and 21st March 1946 – Morning & Afternoon

As Jackson's cross-examination had continued, the atmosphere in the prosecution teams and the press became more and more uneasy. Jackson was failing to lay specific criminal acts at Goering's door. Worse than that, his failure was building Goering's status. There was a fear that ex-Nazis throughout Germany would be watching Goering's performance and taking heart.

Jackson, as the chief American prosecutor, had taken charge of the cross-examination. He should deal with all the major criminality that may have included Goering. The other national prosecutors were expected to ask only supplementary questions, focussing on events that concerned their own national interests.

Under the procedural rules of the Tribunal, no subsequent cross-examiner of Goering could cover the issues that Jackson had already raised. This meant that important topics Jackson had not dealt with in depth – such as the invasion of Poland, the Night of the Long Knives, and Krystallnacht – were off limits. The opportunity to pin Hitler's deputy to these major crimes had been missed.

With Goering dominating his chief cross-examiner, something would have to be done by the other prosecutors to ensure that Goering was definitively linked to at least some of the Third Reich's criminality. Maxwell-Fyfe and his team had planned to concentrate only on the escape of Allied airmen from Stalag Luft III at the end of March 1944 (popularly known as The Great Escape). Now they would have to find other lines of questioning to strengthen their case.

When Jackson wrapped up his questioning, the afternoon session had nearly ended. The session was extended for half an hour, and Maxwell-Fyfe began his cross examination.

Maxwell-Fyfe's questioning in the forty minutes at the end of the afternoon of 20th March concentrated on the execution of Allied airmen who had escaped from prisoner of war camps and been recaptured. The difference in the style of examination was immediately plain. Maxwell-Fyfe's questions were direct, and limited to precise points. He had studied the case documents closely and had them at his fingertips. He understood their context and had learned the correct German titles of men and offices. He could drop names like Zentralluftwaffengericht and Kriegsgefangenenwesen into his questions with confidence.

The questions fixed a trail of events step by step, but it was not easy to understand in advance where he wished to lead his witness. He was not above dissembling; for instance, given his meticulous preparation, it is hard to believe he had not checked the date of Easter in 1944 (it fell on April 9th). Goering stated he had returned from leave a few days before Easter and this date was crucial to gaining his admission that he was in his office and in charge while fifty officers of the Royal Air Force were shot for attempting to escape.

Testimony - Afternoon Session (continued) – 20th March 1946

Maxwell-Fyfe I want to ask you first some questions about the matter of the British Air Force officers who escaped from Stalag Luft III. Do you remember that you said in giving your evidence that you knew this incident very completely and very minutely? Do you remember saying that?

Goering No -- that I had received accurate knowledge; not that I had accurate knowledge -- but that I received it.

Maxwell-Fyfe Let me quote your own words, as they were taken down, "I know this incident very completely, very minutely, but it came to my attention, unfortunately, at a later period of time." That is what you said the other day, is that right?

Goering Yes, that is what I meant; that I know about the incident exactly, but only heard of it 2 days later.

Maxwell-Fyfe You told the Tribunal that you were on leave at this time, in the last period of March 1944, is that right?

Goering Yes, as far as I remember I was on leave in March until a few days before Easter.

Maxwell-Fyfe And you said, "As I can prove." I want you to tell the Tribunal the dates of your leave.

Goering I say again, that this refers to the whole of March -- I remember it well -- and for proof I would like to mention the people who were with me on this leave.

Maxwell-Fyfe What I want to know is, where you were on leave?

Goering Here, in the vicinity of Nuremberg.

Maxwell-Fyfe So you were within easy reach of the telephone from the Air Ministry or, indeed, from Breslau, if you were wanted?

Goering I would have been easily accessible by phone if someone wanted to communicate with me.

Maxwell-Fyfe I want you to help me with regard to one or two other dates of which you have spoken. You say: "I heard 1 or 2 days later about this escape." Do you, understand, Witness, that it is about the escape I am asking you, not about the shooting, for the moment; I want to make it quite clear.

Goering It is clear to me.

Maxwell-Fyfe Did you mean by that, that you heard about the actual escape 1 or 2 days after it happened?

Goering Yes.

Maxwell-Fyfe Did you hear about it from the office of your adjutant or from your director of operations?

Goering I always heard these things through my adjutant. Several other escapes had preceded this one.

Maxwell-Fyfe Yes, that's right. There had been a number of escapes from this camp.

Goering I cannot tell you exactly whether they were from this camp. Shortly before several big escapes had taken place, which I always heard of through the office of my adjutant.

Maxwell-Fyfe I want you to tell the Tribunal another date: you say that on your return from leave your chief of staff made a communication to you. Who was your chief of staff?

Goering General Korten was chief of staff at that time.

Maxwell-Fyfe Can you tell us the date at which he made this communication to you?

Goering No, I cannot tell you that exactly. I believe I discussed this incident with my chief of staff later, telling him what I had already heard about it from other sources.

Maxwell-Fyfe Who was the first to tell you about it? Was it your chief of staff who told you about the shootings? Do you mean that someone else had told you about the shooting?

Goering I cannot say exactly now whether I heard about the shooting from the chief of staff, or from other sources. But in any event I discussed this with the chief of staff.

Maxwell-Fyfe What was the date that you talked about it with your chief of staff?

Goering I cannot tell you the date exactly from memory, but it must have been around Easter.

Maxwell-Fyfe That would be just about the end of March, wouldn't it?

Goering No. It might have been at the beginning of April, the first half of April.

Maxwell-Fyfe And then you had an interview with Himmler, you have told us?

Goering Yes, I talked with Himmler about this.

Maxwell-Fyfe Can you fix that?

Goering Of course I cannot establish this date with certainty. I saw Himmler, and, at the first opportunity after I had heard about this incident, spoke to him about it.

Maxwell-Fyfe So that you can't fix the date in relation to your coming back from leave, or the interview with your chief of staff, or any other date, or Easter?

Goering Without any documents it is, as I said, impossible for me today to fix the date. I can only mention the approximate period of time; and that I have done.

Maxwell-Fyfe You said the other day that you could prove when you were on leave. Am I to take it that you haven't taken the trouble to look up what your leave dates were?

Goering I have already said that I was on leave during March. Whether I returned on the 26th or the 28th or the 29th of March I cannot tell you. For proof of that you would have to ask the people who accompanied me, who perhaps can fix this date more definitely. I know only that I was there in March.

Maxwell-Fyfe Witness, will it be perfectly fair to you if I take the latest of your dates, the 29th of March, to work on?

Goering It would be more expedient if you would tell me when Easter was that year, because I do not recall it. Then it will be easier for me to specify the dates, because I know that a few days before Easter I returned to Berchtesgaden in order to pass these holidays with my family.

Maxwell-Fyfe A few days before Easter you went back to Berchtesgaden?

Goering Yes.

Maxwell-Fyfe So you had come back on leave some day before that. Before you went to Berchtesgaden you had come back from your March leave?

Goering Berchtesgaden was then at the same time the headquarters of the Fuehrer. I returned from, my leave to Berchtesgaden, and with my return my leave ended, because I returned to duty. The return to Berchtesgaden was identical with the termination of my leave.

Maxwell-Fyfe Well, I can't give you Easter offhand, but I happen to remember Whitsuntide was the 28th of May, so that Easter would be early, somewhere about the 5th of April. So that your leave would finish somewhere about the end of March, maybe the 26th or the 29th; that is right, isn't it?

Now, these shootings of these officers went on from the 25th of March to the 13th of April; do you know that?

Goering I do not know that exactly.

Maxwell-Fyfe You may take that from me, because there is an official report of the shooting, and I want to be quite fair with you. Only 49 of these officers were shot on the 6th of April, as far as we can be sure, and one was shot either on the 13th of April or later. But the critical period is the end of March, and we may take it that you were back from leave by about the 29th of March.

I just want you to tell the Tribunal this was a matter of great importance, wasn't it? Considered a matter of great importance?

Goering It was a very important matter.

Maxwell-Fyfe General Milch -- I beg pardon -- Field Marshal Milch has said that it was a matter which would require the highest authority, and I think you have said that you know it was Hitler's decision that these officers should be shot; is that so?

Goering The question did not come through clearly.

Maxwell-Fyfe It was Hitler's decision that these officers should be shot?

Goering That is correct; and I was later notified that it was Hitler's decree.

Maxwell-Fyfe I want you just to remember one other thing, that immediately it was published, the British Foreign Secretary, Mr. Eden, at once said that Great Britain would demand justice of the perpetrators of these murders; do you remember that?

Goering I cannot remember the speech to the House of Commons given by Eden. I myself do not know the substance of this speech even today. I just heard that he spoke in Parliament about this incident.

Maxwell-Fyfe I want you to tell the Tribunal just who the persons in your ministry involved were. I will tell you; I think it would be shorter in the end. If you disagree you can correct me.

The commandant of Stalag Luft III was Oberst Von Lindeiner of your service, was he not?

Goering That is quite possible. I did not know the names of all these commandants. There was a court martial against him and that was because the escape was possible. He was not connected with the shootings.

Maxwell-Fyfe No, but he was commandant of the camp, and I suppose you had to review and confirm the proceedings of the Zentralluftwaffengericht which convicted him and sentenced him to a year's imprisonment for neglect of duty. That would come to you, wouldn't it? Wouldn't that come to you for review?

Goering No, only if larger penalties were involved. One year imprisonment would not come to my attention. But I know, and would like to certify, that court proceedings were taken against him for neglect of duty at the time of the escape.

Maxwell-Fyfe In May of 1943, Inspectorate Number 17 had been interposed between the Luftwaffe and the Prisoners of War Organization of the OKW, the Kriegsgefangenenwesen; do you remember that?

Goering I do not know the details about inspection nor how closely it concerned the Prisoners of War Organization of the OKW or how it was otherwise.

Maxwell-Fyfe I want to remind you of who your own officers were. You understand, Witness, that your own officers are involved in this matter. I want to remind you who they were. Was the head of Inspectorate 17 Major General Grosch of the Luftwaffe?

Goering Major General Grosch is of the Luftwaffe.

Maxwell-Fyfe You told the Tribunal the other day -- I am quoting your own words -- that you knew from information, you knew this incident very completely and very minutely. You are now telling the Tribunal you don't know whether Major General Grosch was head of Inspectorate Number 17 of the Luftwaffe.

Goering That is irrelevant. I told the High Tribunal that I heard an accurate account of the incident of the shooting of these airmen, but that has no connection with General Grosch and his inspectorate, for he did not participate in the shooting.

Maxwell-Fyfe I will show you that connection in one minute if you will just answer my questions. Was Grosch's second in command Oberst Welder; do you remember that?

Goering I do not know the particulars of the organization for inspection of prisoner-of-war camps, nor the leaders, nor what positions they held. At least not by heart. I would like to emphasize again, so that there will be no confusion, that when I said I knew about this matter, I meant that I knew how the order was issued and that the people were shot, that I came to know all about this; but not as far as this was related to inspections, possibilities of flight, *et cetera*.

Maxwell-Fyfe And did General Grosch, as head of Inspectorate 17, have to report to General Forster, your director of operations at the Luftwaffe Ministerium?

Goering That I cannot tell you without having the diagram of the subordinate posts before me. General Forster was, I believe at that time, head of the Luftwehr, or a similar designation, in the ministry. I concerned myself less with these matters, because they were not directly of a tactical, strategic, or of an armament nature. But it is quite possible, and certain that he belonged to this department.

Maxwell-Fyfe I put it to you quite shortly, and if you don't know I will leave it for the moment. Did you know Major General Von Graevenitz was head of the Defendant Keitel's department, the Kriegsgefangenenwesen, that dealt with prisoners of war?

Goering I first heard about General Graevenitz here, for this department did not directly concern me. I could not know all of these military subordinate commanders in their hundreds and thousands of departments.

Maxwell-Fyfe So I take it that you did not know Colonel, now General Westhoff, of the department under Von Graevenitz?

Goering Westhoff I never saw at all, and he did not belong to the Luftwaffe.

Maxwell-Fyfe I am not suggesting that Von Graevenitz and Westhoff belonged to the Luftwaffe. I wanted to make it clear that I was suggesting they belonged to General Keitel's organization.

Goering I did not know either; and I did not know what posts they occupied.

Maxwell-Fyfe Up to that time you still had a considerable influence in the Reich, didn't you?

Goering At this time no longer. This no longer concerns 1944.

Maxwell-Fyfe But you were still head of the Luftwaffe and head of the Air Ministry, weren't you?

Goering Yes, I was.

Maxwell-Fyfe And you had, as head of the Luftwaffe and head of the Air Ministry, been responsible for six prisoner-of-war camps for the whole of the war up to that time, hadn't you?

Goering How many prisoner-of-war camps I do not know. But of course I bear the responsibility for those which belonged to my ministry.

Maxwell-Fyfe To the Air Force?

Goering Yes, those which were subordinate to the Air Force.

Maxwell-Fyfe You knew about the general plan for treatment of prisoners of war, which we have had in evidence as the "Aktion Kugel" plan, didn't you?

Goering No. I knew nothing of this action. I was not advised of it.

Maxwell-Fyfe You were never advised of Aktion Kugel?

Goering I first heard of Aktion Kugel here; saw the document and heard the expression for the first time. Moreover no officer of the Luftwaffe ever informed me of such a thing; and I do not believe that a single officer was ever taken away from the Luftwaffe camps. A report to this effect was never presented to me, in any case.

Maxwell-Fyfe You know what Aktion Kugel was: that escaped officers and non-commissioned officers, other than British and American, were to be handed over to the police and taken to Mauthausen, where they were shot by the device of having a gun concealed in the measuring equipment when they thought they were getting their prison clothes. You know what Aktion Kugel is, don't you?

Goering I heard of it here.

Maxwell-Fyfe Are you telling the Tribunal that you did not know that escaped prisoners of war who were picked up by the police were retained by the police and taken to Mauthausen?

Goering No, I did not know that. On the contrary, various prisoners who escaped from my camps were caught again by the police; and they were all brought back to the camps; this was the first case where this to some extent did not take place.

Maxwell-Fyfe But didn't you know that Colonel Welder, as second in command of your ministry's inspectorate, issued a written order a month before this, in February 1944, that prisoners of war picked up by the Luftwaffe should be delivered back to their camp, and prisoners of war picked up by the police should be held by them and no longer counted as being under the protection of the Luftwaffe; didn't you know that?

Goering No. Please summon this colonel to testify if he ever made a report of that nature to me, or addressed such a letter to me.

Maxwell-Fyfe Well, of course I cannot tell whether your ministry was well run or not. But he certainly issued the order, because he says so himself.

Goering Then he must say from whom he received this order.

Maxwell-Fyfe I see. Well, he says that he issued this order, and you know as well as I do that prisoners of war is a thing that you have got to be careful about, because you have got a protecting power that investigates any complaint; and you never denounced the Convention and you had the protecting power in these matters all through the war, had you not? That is right, isn't it?

Goering That is correct, but I take the liberty to ask who gave him this order, whether he received this order from me.

Maxwell-Fyfe Well, he would not get it direct from you. I do not think you had ever met him, had you? He would get it from Lieutenant General Grosch, wouldn't he?

Goering Then Grosch should say whether he received such an order from me. I never gave such an order.

Maxwell-Fyfe I see. So you say that you had never heard -- this was 3½ years after the beginning of the war -- and you had never heard that any escaped prisoners of war were to be handed over to the police. Is that what you ask the Tribunal to believe?

Goering To the extent that escaped prisoners of war committed any offenses or crimes, they were of course turned over to the police, I believe. But I wish to testify before the Court that I never gave any order that they should be handed over to the police or sent to concentration camps merely because they had attempted to break out or escape, nor did I ever know that such measures were taken.

Maxwell-Fyfe This is my last question: I want to make it quite clear, Witness, that I am referring to those who had escaped, who had got away from the confines of the camp and were recaptured by the police. Didn't you know that they were handed over to the police?

Goering No. Only if they had committed crimes while fleeing, such as murder and so on. Such things occurred.

[The Tribunal adjourned until 21 March 1946 at 1000 hours.]

Morning Session – 21st March 1946

Maxwell-Fyfe began the day's questioning with the Royal Air Force officers who were executed after escaping from Stalag Luft III (now popularly known as The Great Escape). He concentrated on persons and dates, and showed that Goering, despite his denials, had been involved in the murder of these prisoners. This was definitely a war crime, and Maxwell-Fyfe needed to show that Goering had been involved in it.

The questioning then moved on to the question of the planning of Nazi aggression against other countries and started with the invasion of Poland. Here Maxwell-Fyfe was able to use the testimony of Goering's own witness Dahlerus to show Goering had been a part of planning the invasion of Poland at the same time he had been pretending to negotiate with the British government. To complete his coverage of the charges of waging, and conspiracy to wage, aggressive war, Maxwell-Fyfe moved on to the invasions of Holland, Belgium, Yugoslavia and Greece.

The morning ended with a topic that has become a cause of frustration over the years. Many Germans, including Goering, claimed not to have known what was happening in the death camps. Today's best estimate of the number civilians deliberately murdered by the Nazis is about eleven million, of whom a little more than half were Jewish.

It stretched credulity to hear Goering and other defendants claim they knew nothing of the murders, and Maxwell-Fyfe started to demolish Goering's claims.

Testimony - Morning Session – 21st March 1946

Maxwell-Fyfe Witness, do you remember telling me last night that the only prisoners of war handed over to the police were those guilty of crimes or misdemeanors?

Goering I did not express myself that way. I said if the police apprehended prisoners of war, those who had committed a crime during the escape, as far as I know, were detained by the police and were not returned to the camp. To what extent the police kept prisoners of war, without returning them to a camp, I was able to gather from interrogations and explanations here.

Maxwell-Fyfe Would you look at Document D-569? Would you look first at the top left-hand corner, which shows that it is a document published by the Oberkommando der Wehrmacht?

Goering The document which I have before me has the following heading at the top left-hand corner: "The ReichsFuehrer SS," and the subheading: "Inspector of Concentration Camps."

Maxwell-Fyfe It is a document dated the 22d of November 1941. Have you got it?

Goering Yes, I have it now.

Maxwell-Fyfe Now, look at the left-hand bottom corner, as to distribution. The second person to whom it is distributed is the Air Ministry and Commander-in-Chief of the Air Force on 22 November 1941. That would be you.

Goering That's correct. I would like to make the following statement in connection with this ...

Maxwell-Fyfe Just for a moment. I would like you to appreciate the document and then make your statement upon it. I shall not stop you. I want you to look at the third sentence in Paragraph 1. This deals with Soviet prisoners of war, you understand. The third sentence says:

"If escaped Soviet prisoners of war are returned to the camp in accordance with this order, they have to be handed over to the nearest post of the Secret State Police, in any case."

And then Paragraph 2 deals with the special position -- if they commit crimes, owing to the fact that:

"... at present these misdemeanors on the part of Soviet prisoners of war are particularly frequent, due most likely to living conditions still being somewhat unsettled, the following temporary regulations come into force. They may be amended later. If a Soviet prisoner of war commits any other punishable offense then the commandant of the camp must hand the guilty man over to the head of the Security Police."

Do I understand this document to say that a man who escapes will be handed over to the Security Police? You understand this document says a man who escapes will be handed over to the Secret Police, a man who commits a crime, as you mentioned, will be handed over to the Security Police. Wasn't that the condition that obtained from 1941 up to the date we are dealing with in March 1944?

Goering I would like to read the few preceding paragraphs so that no sentences are separated from their context.

Maxwell-Fyfe My Lord, while the witness is reading the document, might I go over the technical matter of the arrangement of exhibits? When I cross-examined Field Marshal Kesselring I put in three documents, UK-66, which becomes Exhibit GB-274; D-39, which becomes GB-275; TC-91, which becomes GB-276; so this document will become GB-277.

[Turning to the witness.] Have you had an opportunity of reading it, Witness?

Goering Yes, I have.

Maxwell-Fyfe Then I am right, am I not, that the Soviet prisoners of war who escaped were to be, after their return to the camp, handed over to the Secret State Police. If they committed a crime, they were to be handed over to the Security Police, isn't that right?

Goering Not exactly correct. I would like to point to the third sentence in the first paragraph. There it says, "If a prisoner-of-war camp is in the vicinity, then the man who is recaptured is to be transported there."

Maxwell-Fyfe But read the next sentence, "If a Soviet prisoner of war is returned to the camp" -- that is in accordance with this order which you have just read -- "he has to be handed to the nearest service station of the Secret State Police." Your own sentence.

Goering Yes, but the second paragraph which follows gives an explanation of frequent criminal acts of Soviet prisoners of war, *et cetera*, committed at that time. You read that yourself; that is also connected with this Paragraph Number 1. But this order was given by itself and it was distributed to the Army, the Air Force and the Navy. And I would like to give the explanation of distribution. In this war there were not only hundreds, but thousands of current orders which were issued by superiors to subordinate officers and were transmitted to various departments.

That does not mean that each of these thousands of orders was submitted to the Commander-in-Chief; only the most decisive and most important were shown to him. The others went from department to department. Thus it is, that this order from the Chief the High Command was signed by a subordinate department, and not by the Chief of the High Command himself.

Maxwell-Fyfe This order would be dealt by your prisoner-of-war department in your ministry, wouldn't it?

Goering This department, according to the procedure adopted for these orders, received the order, but no other department received it.

Maxwell-Fyfe I think the answer to my question must be "yes." It would be dealt with by the prisoner-of-war department -- your ministry. Isn't that so?

Goering I would say yes.

Maxwell-Fyfe It is quicker, you see, if you say "yes" in the beginning; do you understand?

Goering No; it depends upon whether I personally have read the order or not, and I will then determine as to my responsibility.

Maxwell-Fyfe Well now, the escape...

President You were not asked about responsibility you were asked whether it would be dealt with by your prisoner-of-war department.

Maxwell-Fyfe Now, the escape about which am asking you took place on the night of the 24th to the 25th March. I want you to have that date in mind. The decision to murder these young officers must have been taken very quickly because the first murder which actually took place was on the 26th of March. Do you agree with that? It must have been taken quickly?

Goering I assume that this order, as I was informed later, was given immediately, but it had no connection with this document.

Maxwell-Fyfe No, no; we are finished with that document; we are going into the murder of these young men. The Grossfahndung -- a general hue and cry, I think, would be the British translation -- was also issued at once in order that these me should be arrested; isn't that so?

Goering That is correct. Whenever there was an escape, and such a large number of prisoners escaped, automatically in the whole Reich, a hue and cry was raised, that is, all authorities had to be on the lookout to recapture the prisoners.

Maxwell-Fyfe So that in order to give this order to murder these men, and for the Grossfahndung, there must have been a meeting of Hitler, at any rate with Himmler or Kaltenbrunner, in order that that order would be put into effect; isn't that so?

Goering That is correct. According to what I heard, Himmler was the first to report this escape to the Fuehrer.

Maxwell-Fyfe Now, General Westhoff, who was in Defendant Keitel's Kriegsgefangenenwesen, in his prisoner-of-war set-up, says this, that

"On a date, which I think was the 26th, Keitel said to him, 'This morning Goering reproached me in the presence of Himmler for having let some more prisoners of war escape. It was unheard of.'"

Do you say that General Westhoff is wrong?

Goering Yes. This is not in accordance with the facts. General Westhoff is referring to a statement of Field Marshal Keitel. This utterance in itself is illogical, for I could not accuse Keitel because he would not draw my attention to it, as the guarding was his responsibility and not mine.

Maxwell-Fyfe One of the Defendant Keitel's officers dealing with this matter was a general inspector, General Rottich. I do not know if you know him.

Goering No.

Maxwell-Fyfe Well, General Westhoff, as one could understand, is very anxious to assure everyone that his senior officer had nothing to do with it, and he goes on to say this about General Rottich:

"He was completely excluded from it by the fact that these matters were taken out of his hands. Apparently at that conference with the Fuehrer in the morning, that is to say, the conference between Himmler, Field Marshal Keitel, and Goering, which took place in the Fuehrer's presence, the Fuehrer himself always took a hand in these affairs when officers escaped."

You say that is wrong? You were at no such conference?

Goering I was not present at this conference, neither was General Westhoff; he is giving a purely subjective view, not the facts of the case.

Maxwell-Fyfe So that we find that -- you think that -- Westhoff is wrong? You see, Westhoff, he was a colonel at this time, I think, and now he finishes as a major general, and he asks that the senior officers be asked about it; he says this: "It should be possible to find out that Himmler made the suggestion to the Fuehrer -- to find that out from Goering who was present at the conference." Again and again Westhoff, who after all is a comparatively junior officer, is saying that the truth about this matter can be discovered from his seniors. You say that it cannot.

Goering I would not say that. I would like just to say that General Westhoff was never present for even a moment, therefore he cannot say, I know or I saw that Reich Marshal Goering was present. He is assuming it is so, or he may have heard it.

Maxwell-Fyfe What he says is, you know, that Keitel blamed him, as I have read to you; that Keitel went on to say to him at General Von Graevenitz', "Gentlemen, the escapes must stop. We must set an example. We shall take very severe measures. I am only telling you that, that the men who have escaped will be shot; probably the majority of them are dead already." You never heard anything of that?

Goering I was neither present at the Keitel-Westhoff-Graevenitz conversation nor at the Fuehrer-Himmler conversation. As far as I know General Westhoff will be testifying here. Moreover, Field Marshal Keitel will be able to say whether I was there or not.

Maxwell-Fyfe Well then, I am bound to put this to you. I come on to your own ministry. I suppose in general you take responsibility for the actions of the officers of your ministry from the rank of field officer and above -- colonels and major generals and lieutenant generals?

Goering If they acted according to my directives and my instructions, yes; if they acted against my directives and instructions, no.

Maxwell-Fyfe Well now, just let us see what happened in your own ministry. You know that -- do you know, that Colonel Walde made a personal investigation of this matter at the camp? Did you know that?

Goering The particulars about this investigation, as I explained yesterday, are unknown to me; I know only that investigations did take place.

Maxwell-Fyfe Now, on the 27th of March, that was a Monday, did you know that there was a meeting in Berlin about this matter? Just let me tell you who were there before you apply your mind to it, so you will know. Your ministry was represented by Colonel Walde, because Lieutenant General Grosch had another meeting, so he ordered his deputy to attend; the Defendant Keitel's organization was represented by Colonel Von Reurmont; the Gestapo was represented by GruppenFuehrer Muller; the Kripo was represented by GruppenFuehrer Nebe. Now, all these officers were of course not on the policy level, but they were high executive officers who had to deal with the actual facts that were carried out, were they not?

Goering They were not executive officers, insofar as it has not been definitely established that executive powers are within an officer's province. To the first question, whether I knew about this meeting, I would say no. Colonel Walde I do not even know personally.

Maxwell-Fyfe You mean to say, you are telling the Tribunal, that you were never told about this meeting at any time?

Goering Yes, I am saying that.

Maxwell-Fyfe I just want you to look at -- let him have Walde's statement -- I want you to look at the statement of one of the officers of your own ministry on this point. This is a statement made by Colonel Ernst Walde, and -- I am sorry I have not another German copy, but I will get one in due course - and in my copy, Witness, it is at the foot of Page 2, the beginning of the paragraph which I want you to look at, is: "As recaptured prisoners were not to be taken back to their camp, according to an order issued several weeks previously.. ." -- can you find it?

Goering Where is it?

Maxwell-Fyfe Well, in the English version it is at the middle of the second page, and I want to ask you about the -- the middle of that paragraph; I do not know if you see a name -- it stands out in my copy -- Major Dr. Huhnemorder; do you see that?

Goering Yes, I have found it.

Maxwell-Fyfe Well, it is the sentence after the name Major Dr. Huhnemorder appears: "On this Monday" -- have you got this?

Goering Yes.

Maxwell-Fyfe Thank you.

"On this Monday a conference took place at the Reich Security Main Office at Berlin, Albrechtstrasse. As far as I remember this conference had been called by the Chief of the Prisoner-of-War Organization OKW, and I attended as representative of Luftwaffe Inspektion 17, since General Grosch was unable to attend in person, for reasons which I cannot remember; the Chief of the Prisoner-of-War Organization, as far as I know, was represented by Colonel Von Reurmont, while the Security Office was represented by GruppenFuehrer Muller and GruppenFuehrer Nebe, the Chief of the Criminal Police at that time.

"I find it impossible to give a verbatim account of the conversation or to state what was said by every single person. But I remember this much: That we were informed about a conference which had taken place on the previous day, that is Sunday, at the Fuehrer's headquarters in connection with the mass escape from Sagan, in the course of which heated discussions had taken place between the participants.

"In this connection the names of Himmler, Goering, and Keitel were mentioned. Whether Ribbentrop's name was also mentioned I do not remember. The Fuehrer was not mentioned.

"At this conference appropriate measures were said to have been discussed, or taken, to check any such mass escapes in the future. The nature of these measures was not disclosed. Later, and more or less in conclusion, GruppenFuehrer Muller declared that requisite orders had already been given and put into effect the previous morning. Regarding the search for escaped prisoners, he could or would not make any statement; he merely declared that according to reports so far received, shootings had taken place at some points for attempted escapes. I think he said that the number was 10 or 15.

"After these remarks by GruppenFuehrer Muller, which unmistakably caused a shattering effect, it became clear to me that a decision had been made by the highest authority, and that therefore any intervention by subordinate departments was impossible and pointless."

Now, this was announced at a meeting of persons that I would call executives, that the shooting had already begun. Are you telling this Tribunal that this matter was made clear to these executives, including one of your own officers, and was never told to you? Are you still saying that?

Goering I am still saying that. Firstly, that I have never heard anything about this conference. Secondly, that the officer in question is only surmising when he mentions the names, he makes no assertion. And thirdly, I would like to ask you also to mention the beginning of this statement, which begins as follows:

"In this matter of the mass escape of British Air Force officers from Prisoner-of-War Camp Number III, at Sagan on 24 or 25 March 1944, I make the following statement:

"I have to point out that in view of the absence of any documents, I am forced to reconstruct completely from memory events which happened almost a year and 9 months ago; I therefore ask that this fact and the possibility thus arising of my making a mistake be taken into consideration, and that due allowances be made."

Maxwell-Fyfe That is a perfectly fair point, and the answer to it is that I will show you what this officer reported at the time to his general.

Give the witness General Grosch's statement.

[The document was submitted to the witness.] We are getting reasonably high up. This officer, General Grosch, signs it as a Lieutenant General. Now, would you like, if you can, to help me again -- you were most helpful last time -- to try to find the place? This is a statement by Lieutenant General Grosch.

Goering I request to have permission to read this document first, to see whether similar modifications apply here also.

Maxwell-Fyfe Will you read the first sentence? I do not want to take up time to read an account of the general matter. It says: "During my interrogation on 7 December 1945 1 was told to write down all I knew about the Sagan case." And then he wrote it down. But I would like you to look at Number 1, the first page. Do you see at the foot of the page an account of the pyramid in your ministry of administration? Do you see that at the foot of Page 1?

[There was no response.]

Maxwell-Fyfe Witness, do you see at the foot of Page 1 the pyramid?

Goering I see it but -- I am now at the place.

Maxwell-Fyfe It comes in about the fourth paragraph.

Goering I can see it, but I should like to read the other first.

Maxwell-Fyfe Then, if you will look about four small paragraphs on, it begins: "A few days after the day of the escape -- I cannot remember the date any more -- Colonel Walde informed me that

OKW had called a conference in Berlin."

Do you see that?

I do not mind you running through it quickly, but you may take it that the first two pages are what I said were there, the pyramid of your ministry.

Goering Yes, I have found it. Which paragraph, please?

Maxwell-Fyfe It is Part C, the fourth paragraph, the Sagan case. "A few days after the escape...." Do you find that?

Goering Yes, I have the place.

Maxwell-Fyfe Thank you.

"A few days after the day of the escape -- I cannot remember the date any more -- Colonel Walde informed me that the OKW had called a conference in Berlin -- I believe on the premises of a high SS and police authority, and that the Inspectorate Number 17 was to send representatives. I should have liked to have gone myself, but had to attend another conference in Berlin, and asked Colonel Walde to attend as representative. After his return Colonel Walde informed me that the spokesman of the OKW had informed them that there was a decision by the Fuehrer to the effect that, on recapture, the escaped British airmen were not to be handed back to the Luftwaffe but were to be shot."

Then missing a paragraph and taking the last line of the next paragraph:

"It is, however, certain that the danger of their being shot was even then clearly recognizable. I asked Colonel Walde whether such a far-reaching decision would be notified in writing to the High Command of the Luftwaffe or the Reich Air Ministry or whether he had been given anything in writing. Colonel Walde gave me to understand that the assembly were told by the spokesman of the OKW, that they would receive nothing in writing, nor was there to be any correspondence on this subject. The circle of those in the know was to be kept as small as possible.

"I asked Colonel Walde whether the spokesman of the OKW had said anything to the effect that the Reich Marshal or the High Command of the Luftwaffe had been informed about the matter. Colonel Walde assured me that the OKW spokesman had told them that the Reich Marshal was informed."

I will not ask you about that for the moment. I want you to look at what your general did. It says:

"Up to the time of Colonel Walde's report, I had not received even so much as a hint anywhere that escaped prisoners of war should be treated in any other way than according to the provisions of the Geneva Convention.

"The same afternoon I rang up my superior officer, the Chief of Air Defence, to ask time for an interview with General der Flieger Forster. This was fixed for the next morning.

"When I came there to report I found General Forster together with his chief of staff. I asked General Forster for permission to speak to him alone and put the facts before him. In conclusion, I expressed the opinion that if the British airmen were to be shot, (a) there would be a breach of the Geneva Convention, (b) reprisal measures endangering the lives of German airmen held by the British as prisoners of war would have to be expected. I asked General Forster to bring the matter to the notice of the Reich Marshal even at this very late stage, and to stress those two points.

"General Forster was immediately prepared to do this. When it came to the choice of the way in which the matter could be brought to the attention of the Reich Marshal, it was decided to report to State Secretary Field Marshal Milch.

"In my presence General Forster rang up the office of the state secretary and obtained the interview at once. General Forster left the room, and while doing so he instructed me to wait for his return in his study. After some time General Forster came back and told me that he had reported the matter to the state secretary and that Field Marshal Milch had made the necessary notes."

Look at the last paragraph:

"I gave Colonel Walde the order, despite the ban by the OKW, to incorporate a detailed written statement about the conference in our records. So far as I know, this was done."

Dr Stahmer Counsel Stahmer on behalf of the Defendant Goering.

We have had submitted here a series of affidavits given by witnesses who are in Nuremberg and who, in my opinion, could be brought as witnesses in person. Because of the importance of this matter, not only for Goering but for other defendants, I object to this procedure, on the assumption that the same rules apply for cross-examination as examination in chief. By that I mean that we should not be satisfied with an affidavit and depend on an affidavit, if the prosecution can, without difficulty, summon the witness in order to have him testify before the Tribunal, so that the Defence may be in position to cross-examine these witnesses.

President Dr. Stahmer, what you have said is entirely inaccurate. The rules with reference to cross-examination are not the same as rules with reference to examination in chief, and what is being done at the present moment is that the Defendant Goering is being cross-examined as to his credit. He has said that he knew nothing about this matter, and he has been cross-examined to prove that he has lied when he said that.

Dr Stahmer Mr. President, according to my opinion the procedure should be that the witness be brought here in person. The fact remains that, in our estimation, a reference to an affidavit is a less desirable means than the personal testimony of a witness, which affords the Defence the possibility of adducing evidence.

President Dr. Stahmer, as I have already pointed out to you, you are quite in error in thinking that the rules for cross-examination are the same as for examination in chief. The witness at the present moment is being cross-examined and is being cross-examined as to credit; that is to say, to prove whether or not he is telling the truth.

As to the calling of this witness -- I think his name is Grosch -- you can apply to call him if you want to do so. That is an entirely different matter.

Dr Stahmer Yes. I quite understand, Mr. President; but I had to have the possibility of calling the people who are mentioned in this affidavit, in case I consider it necessary.

President Well, you can apply to do that.

Maxwell-Fyfe *[Turning to the witness.]* You understand, what I am suggesting to you is that here was a matter which was not only known in the OKW, not only known in the Gestapo and the Kripo, but was known to your own director of operations, General Forster, who told General Grosch that he had informed Field Marshal Milch. I am suggesting to you, that it is absolutely impossible and untrue that in these circumstances you knew nothing about it.

Goering I would like first to establish an entirely different point. In the German interpretation regarding the first objection by Dr. Stahmer, the following came through:

Maxwell-Fyfe The Tribunal does not want you to discuss legal objections.

President Will you please answer the question that is put to you? You have already been told that you must answer a question directly and make any explanation afterwards, and shorten it.

Maxwell-Fyfe Do you still say, in view of that evidence, in view of these statements from the officers of your own ministry, that you knew nothing about this?

Goering Precisely these statements confirm this, and I would like to make a short explanation. You determined a date. You said it was the 27th. But in this statement by Grosch this date is not determined. It says: "A few days after the escape, I do not recall the date, Colonel Walde informed me."

Secondly, it says here that General Forster, who was not chief of my operational branch but chief of another branch of the ministry, mentioned this matter to State Secretary Field Marshal Milch, without referring to the date. General Field Marshal Milch was here as a witness, but unfortunately, he was never questioned as to whether he gave me this report, and at what time, and whether to me direct.

Maxwell-Fyfe Oh yes, he was, and General Field Marshal Milch took the same line as you, that he knew nothing about it, that Forster had never spoken to him. It was asked by my friend, Mr. Roberts, "Didn't General Forster speak to you about it?"

What I am suggesting is that both you and Field Marshal Milch are saying you knew nothing about it, when you did, and are leaving the responsibility on the shoulders of your junior officers. That is what I am suggesting and I want you to understand it.

Goering No, I do not wish to push responsibility on to the shoulders of my subordinates, and I want to make it clear --- that is the only thing that is important to me -- that Field Marshal Milch did not say that he reported this matter to me. And, secondly, that the date when Forster told Milch about this is not established. It could have been quite possible that on the date when this actually happened, the Chief of the General Staff of the Luftwaffe might already have conferred with me about it. The important factor is -- and I want to maintain it -- that I was not present at the time when the command was given by the Fuehrer. When I heard about it, I vehemently opposed it. But at the time I heard of it, it was already too late. That a few were shot later, was not yet known at the time, neither was the exact time of the event. Most of them had been shot already.

Thirdly, those who escaped, and were captured in the direct vicinity of the camp by our guards were returned to the camp and were not handed over. Those prisoners who were captured by the police and the Grossfahndung, and returned to the camp before the Fuehrer had issued the decree, were likewise not handed over and shot.

Maxwell-Fyfe You know that, according to Wielen, who is going to give evidence, the selection of the officers to be shot -- a list as regards the selection of officers to be shot -- a list had been prepared by the camp authorities at the request of Department 5, that is of the RSHA Kripo Department, in which those officers were regarded as disturbing elements -- plotters and escape leaders, having been specifically mentioned. The names were selected either by the commandant or by one of these officers. Thereupon, the shooting of the officers mentioned by name was accordingly ordered by Department 4 of the RSHA and corresponding instructions sent to the Staatspolizei.

Are you telling the Tribunal you did not know that your own officers were selecting the men to be shot on the ground that they were plotters and escape leaders? In any other service in the world, attempt to escape is regarded as a duty of an officer, isn't it, when he is a prisoner of war? Isn't that so?

Goering That is correct, and I have emphasized that. To your first question, I would like to put on record very definitely that we are dealing with the utterances of a man who will be testifying as a witness. As to whether he actually asked for a list and saw a list, his utterance is illogical. There was no selection made for shooting. Those who were captured by the police were shot without exception, and those who had not been returned to the camp. No officers were selected as representing disturbing elements, but those who had returned to the camp were not shot. Those who were recaptured by the police outside the camp were shot without exception, on the orders, of the Fuehrer. Therefore, the utterance is entirely illogical and not in accordance with the facts.

I know nothing about such a list being asked for, nor about the carrying out of such a wish. I personally pointed out to the Fuehrer repeatedly that it is the duty of these officers to escape, and that on their return after the war, they would have to give an account of such attempts, which as far as I can remember should be repeated three times, according to English rules.

Maxwell-Fyfe You remember that the Government of Germany sent an official note about this matter, saying that they had been shot while resisting arrest while trying to escape? Do you remember that?

Goering I heard for the first time that there had been a note to this effect when the reply to it was sent. I had no part in the drawing up of the note. I know of its contents only through the reply, for I happened to be there when the reply came in.

Maxwell-Fyfe I am not at the moment on the point that everyone now admits that the note was a complete and utter lie. I am on the point of the seriousness of this matter. Do you know that General Westhoff says in his statement: "Then, when we read this note to England in the newspaper, we were all absolutely taken aback. We all clutched our heads, mad." According to Mr. Wielen, who will be here, it was a contributory cause for General Nebe of the Kripo, for nights on end, not going to bed but passing the night on his office settee. You will agree, won't you, Witness, that this was a serious and difficult matter? All these officers that had to deal with it found it a serious and difficult matter, isn't that so?

Goering Not only these officers found this matter serious and difficult, but I myself considered it the most serious incident of the whole war and expressed myself unequivocally and clearly on this point, and later, when I learned the contents of the note, I knew that this note was not in accordance with the truth. I gave expression to my indignation, inasmuch as I immediately told my Quartermaster General to direct a letter to the OKW to the effect that we wished to give up the camps for prisoners of war, because under these circumstances, we no longer wished to have anything to do with them.

Maxwell-Fyfe And according to your evidence in chief, what you did was to turn to Himmler, asking him if he had received the order, and then you said,

"I told him what excitement would result in my branch, because we could not understand such measures; and if he had received such orders, he would please inform me before carrying them through so that I would have the possibility to prevent such orders from being carried out, if possible" -- and then you said that you -- "talked to the Fuehrer and that he confirmed that he had given the order and told me why."

You, according to that evidence, still had enough influence in Germany, in your opinion, to stop even Himmler issuing such orders or carrying -- I am sorry, I said "issuing" -- carrying out such orders.

Goering You are giving my statement a completely wrong meaning. I told Himmler plainly that it was his duty to telephone me before the execution of this matter, to give me the possibility, even at this period of my much diminished influence, to prevent the Fuehrer from carrying out this decree. I did not mean to say that I would have been completely successful, but it was a matter of course that I, as Chief of the Luftwaffe, should make it clear to Himmler that it was his duty to telephone me first of all, because it was I who was most concerned with this matter.

I told the Fuehrer in very clear terms just how I felt, and I saw from his answers that, even if I had known of it before, I could not have prevented this decree, and we must keep in mind that two different methods of procedure are in question. The order was not given to the Luftwaffe, that these people were to be shot by the Luftwaffe personnel, but to the police. If the Fuehrer had said to me, "I will persist in this decree which I gave the police," I would not have been able to order the police not to carry through the Fuehrer's decree. Only if this decree had had to be carried out by my men, would it have been possible for me perhaps to circumvent the decree, and I would like to emphasize this point strongly.

Maxwell-Fyfe Well, that may be your view that you could not have got anywhere with the Fuehrer; but I suggested to you that when all these officers that I mentioned knew about it, you knew about it, and that you did nothing to prevent these men from being shot, but co-operated in this foul series of murders.

President Sir David, are you passing from that now?

Maxwell-Fyfe Yes.

President You are putting in evidence these two documents?

Maxwell-Fyfe I am putting them in. I put them to the witness. D-731 will be GB-278, and D-730 will be GB-279.

President And should you not refer perhaps to the second paragraph in 731?

Maxwell-Fyfe Yes.

President It shows that apparently, in the early hours of the 25th of March the matter was communicated to the office of the adjutant of the Reich Marshal -- the second paragraph beginning with "the escape."

Maxwell-Fyfe Yes.

"The escape of about 30 to 40 prisoners, the exact number having to be ascertained by roll call, was reported by telephone from the Sagan Camp to the inspectorate in the early hours of the 25th of March, Saturday morning, and duly passed on in the same way by this office to the higher authorities which were to be informed in case of mass escapes. These were: 1.) the Office of the Adjutant of the Reich Marshal; 2.) the OKW, for directors of these prisoners of war; 3.) the Inspector General of Prisoners of War; and 4.) Director of Operations, Air Ministry."

I am much obliged. You must remember that the witness did not admit yesterday afternoon that the news of the escape had been given to the office of his adjutant.

President Yes.

Maxwell-Fyfe I am much obliged to you.

Goering The escape was communicated to us every time relatively quickly. I should now like to give my view of the statement made by you before that -- it concerns assertions made by you -- but I still maintain that I did not hear about this incident until after it had occurred.

Maxwell-Fyfe I have put my questions on the incident. I pass to another point. I want to ask you two or three questions about the evidence that you gave 2 days ago, dealing with the evidence of your own witness, Herr Dahlerus, who made his first visit to London on the 25th of August 1939, after an interview and a telephone conversation with you on the 24th. I just want you to fix the date because it is sometimes difficult to remember what these dates are. At that time, you were anxious that he should persuade the British Government to arrange a meeting of plenipotentiaries who would deal with the questions of Danzig and the Corridor. Is that right?

Goering That is correct.

Maxwell-Fyfe You knew perfectly well, did you not, that as far as the Fuehrer was concerned, Danzig and the Corridor was not the real matter that was operating in his mind at all. Will you let me remind you what he said on the 23rd of May:

"Danzig is not the subject of the dispute at all; it is a question of expanding our living space in the East, of securing our food supplies, and of the settlement of the Baltic problem."

You knew that, didn't you?

Goering I knew that he had said these things at that time, but I have already pointed out repeatedly that such discussions can only be assessed, if considered in conjunction with the whole political situation. At the moment of these negotiations with England, we were solely concerned with Danzig and the Corridor.

Maxwell-Fyfe Well, you say that despite what Hitler said on the 23rd of May, that at that moment Hitler was only concerned with Danzig and the Corridor? Do you say that seriously?

Goering I maintain in all seriousness that, in the situation as it was at that time, this was really the case. Otherwise it would be impossible to understand any of Hitler's acts. You might just as well take his book *Mein Kampf* as a basis and explain all his acts by it.

Maxwell-Fyfe I am interested in the last week of August at the moment. I want you now just to remember two points on what you said, with regard to Dahlerus, during the morning of the 25th. Do you remember, you had a telephone conversation with him at 11:30 on the 24th? On the 25th, were you sufficiently in Hitler's confidence to know that he was going to proffer the *note verbale* to Sir Neville Henderson, the British Ambassador, on the 25th? Did you know that?

Goering Yes, of course.

Maxwell-Fyfe At that time, when you were sending Dahlerus, and the *note verbale* was being given to the British Ambassador, the arrangement and order was that you were going to attack Poland on the morning of the 26th, wasn't it?

Goering There seems to be a disturbance on the line.

President I think there is some mechanical difficulty. Perhaps it would be a good thing to adjourn for a few minutes.

[A recess was taken.]

Maxwell-Fyfe You told me, Witness, that the arrangements to attack Poland on the morning of the 26th were changed on the evening of the 25th. Before I come to that, I will ask you one or two questions about that.

Goering No, I did not say that.

Maxwell-Fyfe Wait a minute. I am sorry, but that is what I understood you to say.

Goering No. I said explicitly that already on the 25th the attack for the morning of the 26th was cancelled. It is a technical and military impossibility to cancel a large-scale attack of a whole army the evening before an attack. The shortest time required would be from 24 hours to 48 hours.

I expressly mentioned that on the 25th the situation was clear.

Maxwell-Fyfe At the time, you had asked Dahlerus to go to England on the 24th. It was still the plan that the attack would take place on the 26th. Was not your object in sending Dahlerus to have the British Government discussing their next move when the attack took place, in order to make it more difficult for the British Government?

Goering No, I want to emphasize that -- and perhaps I should have the documents for the date -- that when I sent Dahlerus at that time, and when at that moment Sir Neville had been handed a note on behalf of the Fuehrer, the attack for the 26th had been cancelled and postponed.

Maxwell-Fyfe Let me remind you of what you said yourself on the 29th of August:

"On the day when England gave her official guarantee to Poland, it was 5:30 on 25 August, the Fuehrer called me on the telephone and told me he had stopped the planned invasion of Poland. I asked him then whether it was just temporary or for good. He said, 'No, I will have to see whether we can eliminate British intervention.' I asked him, 'Do you think that it will be definite within 4 or 5 days?'"

Isn't that right?

Goering That was what I said, but I did not say that this occurred on the 25th, but when the Fuehrer was clear about the guarantee that was given. I emphasize that once more ...

Maxwell-Fyfe That was what I was quoting to you. When the official guarantee was given, the treaty was signed at 5:30 on the evening of the 25th of August. I am putting your own words to you. It was after that that the Fuehrer telephoned you and told you the invasion was off. Do you wish to withdraw your statement that it was after the official guarantee was given to Poland?

Goering I emphasized once more -- after we knew that the guarantee would be given. It must be clear to you too that if the signing took place at 5:30 p.m. on the 25th, the Fuehrer could know about it only shortly afterwards. Not till then would the Fuehrer have called a conference, and in that case an attack for the 26th could have been called off only during the night of the 25th to 26th. Every military expert must know that that is an absolute impossibility. I meant to say in my statement, "... when it was clear to the Fuehrer that a guarantee was given."

I emphasize once more that I have not seen this record nor sworn to it.

Maxwell-Fyfe I admit that I do not know anything about that. I do not know whether you were still in Hitler's confidence at the time or not. But, wasn't it a fact that Signor Attolico came on the 25th and told Hitler that the Italian Army and Air Force were not ready for a campaign? Were you told that?

Goering Yes, of course I was told that.

Maxwell-Fyfe That was why the orders for the attack were cancelled on the 26th, wasn't it?

Goering No, that is absolutely wrong, because when the question of Italian assistance came up, the fact was that its value was doubted in many quarters. During the tension of the preceding days it became evident that the demands made by the Italians which could not be fulfilled by us were formulated order to keep Italy out of the war. The Fuehrer was convinced that England had only given such a clear-cut guarantee to Poland, because in the meantime the British Government had learned that it was not the intention of Italy to come into the war as a partner of the Axis.

Maxwell-Fyfe I will put to you your own account of what the Fuehrer said. "I will have to see whether we can eliminate British intervention." Isn't it correct that you tried, through Mr. Dahlerus, in every way, to try and eliminate British intervention?

Goering I have never denied that. It was my whole endeavor to avoid war with England. If it had been possible to avoid this war by coming to an agreement with Poland, then that would have been accepted. If the war with England could have been avoided in spite of a war with Poland, then that was my task also. This is clear from the fact that, even after the Polish campaign had started on 1st September 1939 I still made every attempt to avoid a war with England and to keep the war from spreading.

Maxwell-Fyfe In other words, what you were trying to do from the 25th onwards was to get England to try and agree and help the Reich in the return of Danzig and the Polish Corridor, wasn't that right?

Goering That, of course, is quite clearly expressed.

Maxwell-Fyfe Now, you remember the interview with Mr. Dahlerus. It was the interview in which you colored the portions on the map. I only want you to have it in your mind. If I say 11:30 on the 29th of August it will not mean anything to you. I want you to see it so that I can ask you one or two questions about it.

You remember, at that time, that you were upset at the interview which had taken place when Hitler handed Henderson the German reply, and there had been the remark about the ultimatum. Do you remember that?

Goering Yes, of course I was upset, since that had suddenly completely disturbed my whole position.

Maxwell-Fyfe And is this correct? Mr. Dahlerus says on Page 72 of his book that you came out with a tirade, strong words against the Poles. Do you remember that he quotes you as saying: "Wir kennen die Polen"? Do you remember that?

Goering Yes, of course. You must consider the situation at the time. I had heard about the excesses and I would not go and tell Dahlerus, a neutral, that I considered Germany wholly guilty and the Poles completely innocent. It is correct that I did say that, but it arose out of a situation.

Maxwell-Fyfe Are you still an admirer of Bismarck?

Goering I admire Bismarck absolutely, but I have never said that I am a Bismarck.

Maxwell-Fyfe No, I am not suggesting that. I thought you might have in mind his remark about the Poles. Do you remember: "Haut doch die Polen, dass sie am Leben verzagen"? (Let us strike the Poles until they lose the courage to live.) Is that what was in your mind at the time?

Goering No, I had no such thoughts, still less because for years I had genuinely sought friendship with Poland.

Maxwell-Fyfe You have been quite frank about your general intention, and I am not going to take time on it, but I just want to put one or two subsidiary points.

You remember the passage that I read from Mr. Dahlerus' book about the airplane and the sabotage, that he said that you had said to him, mentioning the Defendant Ribbentrop -- you remember that passage? You have given your explanation and I just want to ...

Goering Yes, yes, I gave that explanation and I made it quite clear.

Maxwell-Fyfe Now, your explanation was that Herr Dahlerus was confusing your concern that his airplane should not be shot down in making his journey. That is putting your explanation fairly, isn't it? You are saying that Herr Dahlerus was confused. What you were saying was your concern that his airplane should not be shot down. Isn't that right? That is as I understood it.

Goering No, I think I have expressed it very clearly. Would you like me to give it again? I will repeat it.

Dahlerus, who stood in the witness box here, used the words, "I must correct myself," when he was asked about Ribbentrop. I am quoting Dahlerus. He said, "I connected it with Ribbentrop, since shortly beforehand the name was mentioned in some other connection."

Thereupon I explained I was really anxious lest something might happen. I explained that very clearly and I need not repeat it.

Maxwell-Fyfe The question I put to you, Witness -- I think we are agreed on it -- was that your anxiety was about his plane, and the point that I want to make clear to you now is that that incident did not occur on this day when Dahlerus was preparing for his third visit, but occurred when he was in England and rang you up during his second visit. He rang you up on the evening of the 27th of August, and on Page 59 of his book he says:

"Before leaving the Foreign Office, I telephoned Goering to confirm that I was leaving for Berlin by plane at 7:00 p.m. He seemed to think this was rather late. It would be dark and he was worried lest my plane be shot at by the British, or over German territory. He asked me to hold the line, and a minute later came back and gave me a concise description of the route the plane must follow over Germany to avoid being shot at. He also assured me that the anti-aircraft stations along our course would be informed that we were coming."

What I am suggesting to you is that your explanation is wrong, that you have confused it with this earlier incident of which Mr. Dahlerus speaks, and that Mr. Dahlerus is perfectly accurate when he speaks about the second incident which occurred 2 days later.

Goering That is not at all contradictory. In regard to the first flight the position was that it was already dark, which means that the danger was considerably greater; and I again point out that, in connection with the second journey, preparedness for war in all countries had reached such a degree that flying was hazardous.

I emphasize once more that I had to correct Dahlerus when he was questioned by my counsel, that I did not tell him that Ribbentrop had planned an attack against him. I emphasize for the last time that Von Ribbentrop knew nothing about my negotiations with Dahlerus.

Maxwell-Fyfe Do you really say that? Do you remember that on the 29th of August -- first of all, on the 28th of August, at 10:30 p.m., when Henderson and Hitler had an interview. That was before the difficulties arose. It was the interview when Hitler was considering direct negotiations with the Poles. He said, "We must summon Field Marshal Goering to discuss it with him." That is in our *Blue Book*, and as far as I know it has never been denied. You were summoned to the interview that Hitler and Ribbentrop were having with Sir Neville Henderson.

Goering No, I must interrupt you. The Fuehrer said, "We will have to fetch him," but I was not fetched and that is not said in the Blue Book either.

Maxwell-Fyfe But according to Mr. Dahlerus, he says:

"During our conversation Goering described how he had been summoned to Hitler immediately after Henderson's departure, how Hitler, Goering, and Ribbentrop had discussed the conference that had taken place with Henderson, and how satisfied all three of them were with the result. In this connection Hitler had turned to Ribbentrop and said mockingly, 'Do you still believe that Dahlerus is a British agent?' Somewhat acidly Ribbentrop replied that perhaps it was not the case."

You say that is not true, either?

Goering Herr Dahlerus is describing the events without having been present. From that description, too, it becomes clear that I arrived after Henderson had already left. The description is a little colorful. Ribbentrop had no idea what I was negotiating with Dahlerus about, and the Fuehrer did not inform him about these negotiations either. He merely knew that I used Dahlerus as a negotiator, and he was of course, opposed to him, because he, as Foreign Minister, was against any other channels being used.

Maxwell-Fyfe That was exactly the point, you know, that I put to you about 7 minutes ago, that Ribbentrop did know you were using Dahlerus, with which you disagreed. You now agree that he knew you were using Dahlerus, so I will leave it.

Goering No, I beg your pardon. I still say -- please do not distort my words -- that Ribbentrop did not know what I was negotiating with Dahlerus about, and that he had not even heard of it through the Fuehrer.

Maxwell-Fyfe You said "distort my words." I especially did not say to you that he knew what you were negotiating about. I said to you that he knew you were using Dahlerus, and that, you agree, is right. I limited it to that, didn't I? And that is right, isn't it?

Goering He did not know either that I was carrying on negotiations with England through Dahlerus at that time. He did not know about the flights either.

Maxwell-Fyfe Well now, I want you just to help me on one or two other matters.

You remember that in January of 1937, and in October of 1937, the German Government gave the strongest assurances as to the inviolability and neutrality of Belgium and Holland. Do you remember that?

Goering I do not remember it in detail, but it has been mentioned here in Court.

Maxwell-Fyfe And do you remember that on the 25th of August 1938 the Air Staff put in a memorandum on the assumption that France and Great Britain -- oh no, that France would declare war during the case of Fall Grun, and that Great Britain would come in? Do you remember that? It is Document Number 375-PS, Exhibit Number USA-84. I want you to have it generally in mind because I am going to put a passage to you.

Goering May I ask whether the signature is Wolter? W-o-1-t-e-r?

Maxwell-Fyfe I shall let you know. Yes, that is right.

Goering In that case I remember the document exactly. It has been given to me here.

Maxwell-Fyfe That is right. I only want to recall your recollection to one sentence:

"Belgium and the Netherlands in German hands represent an extraordinary advantage in the prosecution of the air war against Great Britain as well as against France. Therefore, it is held to be essential to obtain the opinion of the Army as to the conditions under which an occupation of this area could be carried out, and how long it would take."

Do you remember that? It is pretty obvious air strategy, but you remember it?

Goering That is absolutely correct. That was the principal work of a captain of the General Staff, 5th Department, who, naturally, when making his report, must propound the best arguments.

Maxwell-Fyfe Then, after that, on the 28th of April 1939, you remember that Hitler said that he had given binding declarations to a number of states, and this applied to Holland and Belgium? I think that was the time when he made a speech in the Reichstag and mentioned a number of small states as well as that; but he said it included Holland and Belgium.

Goering Yes. It has of course been mentioned repeatedly here.

Maxwell-Fyfe Yes. Now, do you remember that on the 23rd of May, in the document that I have already put to you, at the meeting at the Reich Chancellery, Hitler said this: "The Dutch and Belgian air bases must be occupied by armed force. Declarations of neutrality must be ignored."

Do you remember his saying that?

Goering It says so in the document, yes.

Maxwell-Fyfe And, on the 22d of August 1939, in the speech to the commanders-in-chief, which is Document Number 798-PS, Exhibit Number USA-29, he said:

"Another possibility is the violation of Dutch, Belgian, and Swiss neutrality. I have no doubt that all these states, as well as Scandinavia, will defend their neutrality by all available means. England and France will not violate the neutrality of these countries."

Do you remember his saying that?

Goering You can see for yourself from those words how often the Fuehrer changed his ideas, so that even the plan he had in May was not at all final.

Maxwell-Fyfe They are perfectly consistent in my estimation. He is saying that they must be occupied; that declarations of neutrality must be ignored, and he is emphasizing that by saying that England and France will not violate the neutrality, so it is perfectly easy for Germany to do it.

Goering No, what he means to say is that we on our part would not find it necessary to do so either. I merely want to point out that political situations always turn out to be different, and that at these interrogations and this Trial we must regard the political background of the world as a whole.

Maxwell-Fyfe That was on the 22nd. You have agreed as to what was said. Immediately after that, on the 26th, 4 days later, Hitler gave another assurance. Do you remember that, just before the war he gave another assurance?

Goering Yes.

Maxwell-Fyfe And on the 6th of October, 1939, he gave a further assurance, and on the 7th of October, the day after that last assurance, the order, which is Document Number 2329-PS, Exhibit GB-105, was issued.

"Army Group B has to make all preparations according to special orders for immediate invasion of Dutch and Belgian territory, if the political situation so demands."

And on the 9th of October, there is a directive from Hitler:

"Preparations should be made for offensive action on the northern flank of the Western Front crossing the area of Luxembourg, Belgium, and Holland. This attack must be carried out as soon and as forcibly as possible."

Isn't it quite clear from that, that all along you knew, as Hitler stated on the 22nd of August, that England, and France would not violate the neutrality of the low countries, and you were prepared to violate them whenever it suited your strategical and tactical interests? Isn't that quite clear?

Goering Not entirely. Only if the political situation made it necessary. And in the meantime the British air penetration of the neutrality of Holland and Belgium had taken place, up to October.

Maxwell-Fyfe You say not entirely. That is as near agreement with me as you are probably prepared to go.

Now I want to ask you quite shortly again about Yugoslavia. You remember that you have told us in your evidence in chief that Germany before the war, before the beginning of the war, had the very best relations with the Yugoslav people, and that you yourself had contributed to it. I am putting it quite shortly.

Goering That is correct.

Maxwell-Fyfe And that was emphasized, if you will remember, on the first of June 1939 by a speech of Hitler at a dinner with Prince Paul.

Goering Yes.

Maxwell-Fyfe Now, 80 days after that, on the 12th of August 1939, the Defendant Ribbentrop, Hitler, and Ciano had a meeting, and just let me recall to you what Hitler said at that meeting to Count Ciano.

"Generally speaking..."

Goering I beg your pardon, what is the number of the document?

Maxwell-Fyfe I am sorry, it was my fault -- Document Number TC-77, Exhibit Number GB-48. It is the memorandum of a conversation between Hitler, Ribbentrop, and Ciano at Obersalzberg on the 12th of August.

Goering I merely wanted to know if this was from Ciano's diary? That is important for me.

Maxwell-Fyfe Oh no, not from Ciano's diary, it is a memorandum. This is the official report.

"Generally speaking, the best thing to happen would be for uncertain neutrals to be liquidated one after the other. This process could be carried out more easily if on every occasion one partner of the Axis covered the other while it was dealing with an uncertain neutral. Italy might well regard Yugoslavia as a neutral of this kind."

That was rather inconsistent with your statement as to the good intentions towards Yugoslavia, and the Fuehrer's statement to Prince Paul, wasn't it?

Goering I should like to read that through carefully once more and see in what connection that statement was made. As it is presented now it certainly would not fit in with that.

Maxwell-Fyfe You know I do not want to stop you unnecessarily in any way, but that document has been read at least twice during the Trial and any further matter perhaps you will consider. But you will agree, unless I have wrenched it out of its context -- and I hope I have not -- that is quite inconsistent with friendly intentions, is it not?

Goering As I said, it does not fit in with that.

Maxwell-Fyfe Now, it was 56 days after that, on the 6th of October, Hitler gave an assurance to Yugoslavia and he said:

"Immediately after the completion of the Anschluss I informed Yugoslavia that from now on the frontier with this country would also be an unalterable one and that we only desired to live in peace and friendship with her."

And then again in March 1941, on the entry of the Tripartite Pact, the German Government announced that it confirmed its determination to respect the sovereignty and territorial integrity of Yugoslavia at all times.

Now, after that of course, as I have always said when you dealt with this, there was the Simovic Putsch in Yugoslavia. But I think you said quite frankly in your evidence, that Hitler and yourself never took the trouble, or thought of taking the trouble, of inquiring whether the Simovic Government would preserve its neutrality or not. That is right, is it not?

Goering I did not say that. We were convinced that they were using these declarations to mislead. We knew that this Putsch was first of all directed from Moscow, and, as we learned later, that it had been financially supported to a considerable extent by Britain. From that we recognized the hostile intentions as shown by the mobilization of the Yugoslav Army, which made the matter quite clear, and we did not want to be deceived by the Simovic declarations.

Maxwell-Fyfe Well, I would like to say one word about the mobilization in a moment. But on the 27th of March, that was 2 days after the signing of the pact I have just referred to, there was a conference in Berlin of Hitler with the German High Command, at which you were present, and do you remember the Fuehrer saying:

"The Fuehrer is determined, without waiting for possible loyalty declarations of the new government, to make all preparations to destroy Yugoslavia militarily and as a national unit. No diplomatic inquiries will be made nor ultimatums presented. Assurances of the Yugoslav Government, which cannot be trusted anyhow in the future, will be taken note of. The attack will start as soon as means and troops suitable for it are ready. Politically it is especially important that the blow against Yugoslavia is carried out with unmerciful harshness and that the military destruction is effected in a lightning-like undertaking. The plan is on the assumption that we speed up schedules of all preparations and use such strong forces that the Yugoslav collapse will take place within the shortest possible time."

It was not a very friendly intention toward Yugoslavia to have no diplomatic negotiations, not give them the chance of assurance or coming to terms with you, and to strike with unmerciful harshness, was it?

Goering I have just said that after the Simovic Putsch the situation was completely clear to us, and declarations of neutrality on the part of Yugoslavia could be regarded as only camouflage and deception in order to gain time. After the Putsch, Yugoslavia definitely formed part of the enemy front, and it was therefore for us also to carry out deceptive moves and attack as quickly as possible, since our forces at that time were relatively weak.

Maxwell-Fyfe You realized, of course, that you said that General Simovic was inspired by Moscow. I am not going to argue that point with you at all. But I do point out to you that this was 3 months before you were at war with the Soviet Union. You realize that, do you?

Goering Yes, that is correct. It was precisely the Simovic Putsch which removed the Fuehrer's last doubts that Russia's attitude towards Germany had become hostile. This Putsch was the very reason which caused him to decide to take quickest possible counter measures against this danger. Secondly ...

Maxwell-Fyfe Just one moment. Do you know that it appears in the documents quite clearly, that the attack on the Soviet Union was postponed for 6 weeks because of this trouble in the Balkans? That is quite inconsistent with what you are saying now, isn't it?

Goering No. If you will read again my statement on that point, you will see I said that a number of moves on the part of Russia caused the Fuehrer to order preparations for invasion, but that he still withheld the final decision on invasion, and that after the Simovic Putsch this decision was made. From the strategic situation it follows that the military execution of this political decision was delayed by the Yugoslavian campaign.

Maxwell-Fyfe I want to ask you one other point about Yugoslavia.

You remember your evidence that the attack on Belgrade was due to the fact that the war office and a number of other important military organizations were located there. I am trying to summarize it, but that was the effect of your evidence, was it not?

Goering Yes.

Maxwell-Fyfe Now, do you remember how it was put in Hitler's order which I have just been reading to you:

"The main task of the Air Force is to start as early as possible with the destruction of the Yugoslavian Air Force ground installations..."

Now, I ask you to note the next word "and":

"...and to destroy the capital of Belgrade in attacks by waves.

Besides the Air Force has to support the Army."

I put it to you that that order makes it clear that the attack on Belgrade was just another of your exhibitions of terror attacks in order to attempt to subdue a population that would have difficulty in resisting them.

Goering No, that is not correct. The population of Belgrade did defend itself. Belgrade was far more a center of military installations than the capital of any other country; and I would like to draw your attention to this.

Maxwell-Fyfe Well, now, I am going to pass from that matter to one or two points on which you gave evidence -- I think at the instance of counsel for the organizations. You remember you gave evidence in answer to Dr. Babel about the Waffen-SS? Do you remember that -- a few days ago?

Goering Yes.

Maxwell-Fyfe I would just like you to look at a document which has not got a number, but it is the Fuehrer's ideas about the Waffen-SS, and to see if you agree. It is Document Number D-665, and it will be Exhibit Number GB-280. It is a document from the High Command of the Army, General Staff of the Army -- statements of the Fuehrer regarding the future state military police -- and the covering letter of the document says, "After the Fuehrer's proposals for the Waffen-SS had been passed on, doubts arose as to whether it was intended that they should be given wider distribution." If you will pass to the documents, perhaps you will follow it while I read it. I do not think it has been introduced before:

"On 6 August 1940 when the order for the organization of the Leibstandarte Adolf Hitler" -- Adolf Hitler Bodyguard -- was issued, the Fuehrer stated the principles regarding the necessity for the Waffen-SS as summed up below:

"The Greater German Reich in its final form will not include within its frontiers only those national groups which from the very beginning will be well disposed towards the Reich. It is therefore necessary to maintain outside the Reich proper a state military police capable in any situation of representing and imposing the authority of the Reich.

"This task can be carried out only by a state police composed of men of best German blood and wholeheartedly pledged to the ideology on which the Greater German Reich is founded. Only such a formation will resist subversive influences, even in critical times. Such a formation, proud of its purity, will never fraternize with the Proletariat and with the underworld which undermines the fundamental idea. In our future Greater German Reich, a police corps will have the necessary authority over the other members of the community only if it is trained along military lines. Our people are so military minded as a result of glorious achievements in war and training by the National Socialist Party that a 'sock-knitting' police, as in 1848, or a bureaucratic police, as in 1918, would no longer have any authority.

"It is therefore necessary that this state police proves its worth and sacrifices its blood at the front, in close formations, in the same way as every unit of the armed forces. Having returned home, after having proved themselves in the field in the ranks of the Army, the units of the Waffen-SS will possess the authority to execute their tasks as state police.

"This employment of the Waffen-SS for internal purposes is just as much in the interests of the Wehrmacht itself. We must never again allow the conscripted German Wehrmacht to be used against its fellow countrymen, weapon in hand, in critical situations at home. Such action is the beginning of the end. A state which has to resort to such methods is no longer in a position to use its armed forces against an enemy from without, and thereby gives itself up.

"There are deplorable examples of this in our history. In future the Wehrmacht is to be used solely against the foreign enemies of the Reich.

"In order to ensure that the men in the units of the Waffen-SS are always of high quality, the recruitment into the units must be limited. The Fuehrer's idea of this limitation is that the units of the Waffen-SS should generally not exceed 5 to 10 percent of the peacetime strength of the Army."

Do you agree with that? Is that a correct description of the purpose of the Waffen-SS?

Goering I am absolutely convinced that he did say that, but that does not contradict my statement.

Maxwell-Fyfe Now, I just want you, while we are on the SS, to look at a note which is Document D-729 and will be Exhibit Number GB-281. It is on the conversation between you and the Duce in the Palazzo Venezia on 23 October 1942. At that time you were still in good odor with the Fuehrer and still retained your power; is that right?

I will read it: It is Page 35, Paragraph 1.

"The Reich Marshal then described Germany's method in fighting the partisans. To begin with, all livestock and foodstuffs were taken away from the areas concerned, so as to deny the partisans all sources of supply."

Goering Just a second please. Where is this?

Maxwell-Fyfe It is Page 35, Paragraph 1, but I will find it for you if you have any difficulty. I think it is marked, and it begins "The Reich Marshal..." Can you find it?

Goering Yes.

Maxwell-Fyfe I will start again if I may.

"The Reich Marshal then described Germany's method in fighting the partisans. To begin with, all livestock and foodstuffs were taken away from the areas concerned, so as to deny the partisans all sources of supply. Men and women were taken away to labor camps, the children to children's camps, and the villages burned down. It was by the use of these methods that the railways in the vast wooded areas of Bialowiza had been safeguarded.

"Whenever attacks occurred, the entire male population of the villages were lined up on one side and the women on the other. The women were told that all the men would be shot, unless they -- the women -- pointed out which men did not belong to the village. In order to save their men, the women always pointed out the non-residents.

"Germany had found that, generally speaking, it was not easy to get soldiers to carry out such measures. Members of the Party discharged this task much more harshly and efficiently. For the same reason armies trained ideologically, such as the German -- or the Russian -- fought better than others. The SS, the nucleus of the old Party fighters, who have personal ties with the Fuehrer and who form a special elite, confirm this principle."

Now, is that a correct description?

Goering Yes, certainly.

Maxwell-Fyfe And this expresses correctly your views on how war against partisans should be carried out?

Goering I have transmitted this. Just a second, please. May I ask what the number of this document is?

Maxwell-Fyfe Yes, I will give it again: Document Number D-729, and it becomes Exhibit Number GB-281.

Now, I just want you to help me on one other matter on these organizations. You will remember that in answer, I think, to Dr. Servatius, you made some remarks about the Leadership Corps. Do you remember that? I just want you to have them in mind.

Goering Yes.

Maxwell-Fyfe Now, will you look at the document which will be presented to you, Document Number D-728, Exhibit Number GB-282. This is a document from the Office of the Gau Leadership for Hessen-Nassau. I am sorry; there is a reference to an order of the Party Chancellery dated 10 February 1945, its subject is, "Action by the Party to be taken for keeping the German population in check until the end of the war." It is signed by Sprenger, Gauleiter and Commissioner for Reich Defence.

Goering The date is 15 March 1945, is that right?

Maxwell-Fyfe I am grateful to you. I knew it was just after 10 March. I have not got it in my copy, but if you say it, I will take it.

Goering 1945.

Maxwell-Fyfe Yes.

[Sir David Maxwell-Fyfe then read from the document excerpts which were withdrawn and stricken from the record on 16 August 1946.][Author's note: this document was not allowed by the Tribunal because of doubts as to its authenticity.]

Dr Stahmer I must object to the use of this document, since I cannot recognize that it is genuine. I have not yet seen the original, and the doubts as to its being genuine are due to the fact that expressions are used which are most unusual in the German language.

Goering I was going to raise the same objection. It is not an original as it says at the top, "copy," and there is, no original signature, but only the typewritten words "Sprenger, Gauleiter" at the bottom.

Dr Stahmer For instance the expression "Gerichtlichkeiten" is used. This is an expression completely unusual and unknown in the German language, and I cannot imagine that an official document originating from a Gauleiter could contain such a word.

Goering I can draw your attention to yet another point showing that this is evidently not an original document. If there had been an increase in meat or fat rations, I would have heard something about it. Not a single word of these two documents is known to me. It does not bear a rubber stamp either, the whole thing is typewritten, including the signatures. Therefore, I cannot accept this document.

Maxwell-Fyfe This is a file copy which, to the best of my knowledge, was captured at the office of the Gau Leader. It was sent to us by the British Army of the Rhine. I shall make inquiries about it, but it purports to be a file copy and I have put the original document which we have, which is a file copy, to the witness.

President Dr. Stahmer, I have the original document in my hands now, together with the certificate of an officer of the British Army stating that the document was delivered to him in the above capacity, in the ordinary course of official business, as the original of a document found in German records of files captured by military forces under the command of the Supreme Commander. Under these circumstances it is in exactly the same position as all the other captured documents. The defence, of course, can bring any evidence which it thinks right, to criticize the authenticity of the document. The document stands on exactly the same footing as the other captured documents, subject to any criticism to support which you may be able to bring evidence.

Maxwell-Fyfe Witness, I want you to deal with the sentence in paragraph 6.

Now, this paragraph is certainly directed to all administrative levels down to the Kreisleiter, county leaders of the Nazi Party, and it assumes they knew all about the running of concentration camps. Are you telling the Tribunal that you, who up to 1943 were the second man in the Reich, knew nothing about concentration camps?

Goering First of all, I want to say once more that I do not accept this document, and that its whole wording is unknown to me, and that this paragraph appears unusual to me. I did not know anything about what took place and what methods were used in the concentration camps later, when I was no longer in charge.

Maxwell-Fyfe Let me remind you of the evidence that has been given before this Court, that as far as Auschwitz alone is concerned, 4,000,000 people were exterminated. Do you remember that?

Goering This I have heard as a statement here, but I consider it in no way proved -- that figure, I mean.

Maxwell-Fyfe If you do not consider it proved, let me remind you of the affidavit of Hoettl, who was Deputy Group Leader of the Foreign Section, of the Security Section of Amt IV of the RSHA. He says that approximately 4,000,000 Jews have been killed in the concentration camps, while an additional 2,000,000 met death in other ways. Assume that these figures -- one is a Russian figure, the other a

German -- assume they are even 50 percent correct, assume it was 2,000,000 and 1,000,000, are you telling this Tribunal that a Minister with your power in the Reich could remain ignorant that that was going on?

Goering This I maintain, and the reason for this is that these things were kept secret from me. I might add that in my opinion not even the Fuehrer knew the extent of what was going on.

This is also explained by the fact that Himmler kept all these matters very secret. We were never given figures or any other details.

Maxwell-Fyfe But, Witness, haven't you access to the foreign press, the press department in your ministry, to foreign broadcasts? You see, there is evidence that altogether, when you take the Jews and other people, something like 10,000,000 people have been done to death in cold blood, apart from those killed in battle. Something like 10,000,000 people. Do you say that you never saw or heard from the foreign press, in broadcasts, that this was going on?

Goering First of all, the figure 10,000,000 is not established in any way. Secondly, throughout the war I did not read the foreign press, because I considered it nothing but propaganda. Thirdly, though I had the right to listen to foreign broadcasts, I never did so, simply because I did not want to listen to propaganda. Neither did I listen to home propaganda.

Only during the last 4 days of the war did I -- and this I could prove -- listen to a foreign broadcasting station for the first time.

Maxwell-Fyfe You told Mr. Justice Jackson yesterday that there were various representatives in Eastern territories, and you have seen the films of the concentration camps, haven't you, since this Trial started? You knew that there were millions of garments, millions of shoes, 20,952 kilograms of gold wedding rings, 35 wagons of furs -- all that stuff which these people who were exterminated at Maidanek or Auschwitz left behind them. Did nobody ever tell you, under the development of the Four Year Plan, or anyone else, that they were getting all these amounts of human material? Do you remember we heard from the Polish Jewish gentleman, who gave evidence, that all he got back from his family, of his wife and mother and daughter, I think, were their identity cards? His work was to gather up clothes. He told us that so thorough were the henchmen of your friend Himmler that it took 5 minutes extra to kill the women because they had to have their hair cut off as it was to be used for making mattresses. Was nothing ever told you about this accretion to German material, which came from the effects of these people who were murdered?

Goering No, and how can you imagine this? I was laying down the broad outlines for the German economy, and that certainly did not include the manufacture of mattresses from women's hair or the utilization of old shoes and clothes. I leave the figure open. But, also I do want to object to your reference to my "friend Himmler."

Maxwell-Fyfe Well, I will say, "your enemy Himmler," or simply "Himmler", whichever you like. You know whom I mean, don't you?

Goering Yes, indeed.

Maxwell-Fyfe Now, I just want to remind you of one other point: Exhibit Number USA-228, Document Number 407(V)-PS, "...I have the honor to report to you that it was possible to add 3,638,056 new foreign workers to the German war economy between April 1st of last year and March 31st of this year... In addition to the foreign civilian workers 1,622,929 prisoners of war are employed in the German economy."

Now, just listen to this, "out of the 5,000,000 foreign workers who have arrived in Germany, not even 200,000 came voluntarily." That is from the minutes of the Central Planning Board on the 1st of March. Do you say that you, in your position in the State and as the great architect of German economy, did not know that you were getting for your economy 4,800,000 foreign workers who were forced to come? Do you tell the Tribunal that?

Goering I never told the Tribunal that. I said that I knew quite well that these workers were brought in and not always voluntarily, but whether the figure of 200,000 is correct, that I do not know, and I do not believe it either. The number of volunteers was greater, but this does not alter the fact that workers were forced to come to the Reich. That I have never denied, and have even admitted it.

Maxwell-Fyfe You admit -- and I want to put it quite fairly -- that a large number of workers were forced to come to the Reich and work there?

Goering Yes, certainly.

President Sir David, would you like to adjourn now?

Maxwell-Fyfe Yes, sir.

[The Tribunal recessed until 1400 hours.]

Testimony - Afternoon Session – 21st March 1946

Maxwell-Fyfe Do you remember what you said about the relations between you and the Fuehrer? May I repeat your words:

"The chief influence on the Fuehrer, if I may mention influence on the Fuehrer at all, was up to the end of 1941 or the beginning of 1942, and that influence was I. Then my influence gradually decreased until 1943, and from 1943 on it decreased speedily. All in all, apart from myself I do not believe anyone else had anywhere near the influence on the Fuehrer that I had."

That is your view on that matter?

Goering Yes.

Maxwell-Fyfe I think you told the Tribunal that right up to the end your loyalty to the Fuehrer was unshaken, is that right?

Goering That is correct.

Maxwell-Fyfe Do you still seek to justify and glorify Hitler after he had ordered the murder of these 50 young flying officers at Stalag Luft Number III?

Goering I am here neither to justify the Fuehrer Adolf Hitler nor to glorify him. I am here only to emphasize that I remained faithful to him, for I believe in keeping one's oath not in good times only, but also in bad times when it is much more difficult.

As to your reference to the 50 airmen, I never opposed the Fuehrer so clearly and strongly as in this matter, and I gave him my views about it. After that no conversation between the Fuehrer and myself took place for months.

Maxwell-Fyfe The Fuehrer, at any rate, must have had full knowledge of what was happening with regard to concentration camps, the treatment of the Jews, and the treatment of the workers, must he not?

Goering I already mentioned it as my opinion that the Fuehrer did not know about details in concentration camps, about atrocities as described here. As far as I know him, I do not believe he was informed. But insofar as he ...

Maxwell-Fyfe I am not asking about details; I am asking about the murder of four or five million people. Are you suggesting that nobody in power in Germany, except Himmler and perhaps Kaltenbrunner, knew about that?

Goering I am still of the opinion that the Fuehrer did not know about these figures.

Maxwell-Fyfe Now, you remember how Mr. Dahlerus described the relations between you and Hitler on Page 53 of his book:

"From the very beginning of our conversation, I resented his manner towards Goering, his most intimate friend and comrade from the years of struggle. His desire to dominate was explicable, but to require such obsequious humility as Goering now exhibited, from his closest collaborator, seemed to me abhorrent and unprepossessing."

Is that how you had to behave with Hitler?

Goering I did not have to behave in that way, and I did not behave in that way. Those are journalistic statements by Dahlerus, made after the war. If Germany had won the war, this description would certainly have been very different.

Maxwell-Fyfe Mr. Dahlerus was your witness, though.

Goering Mr. Dahlerus was not asked to give a journalistic account. He was solely questioned about the matters with which he, as courier between myself and the British Government, had to deal.

Maxwell-Fyfe My Lord, on Tuesday of last week, the defendant called General Bodenschatz, who gave general evidence as to his character and reputation. He, therefore, in my respectful submission, makes me entitled to put one document to him which is an account by the Defendant Raeder of his general character and reputation. In accordance with the English practice, I make my submission and ask the Court's permission to put it in.

Dr Stahmer I object to the reading of this document. It would be considerably easier to question Admiral Raeder, as witness, on his statements, since he is here with us. Then we shall be able to determine in cross-examination whether and to what extent he still maintains this alleged statement.

Maxwell-Fyfe I have to put it in cross-examination to give the defendant the chance of answering it. The Defendant Raeder can give his explanations when he comes into the witness box.

President The Tribunal would like to look at the document before it is put in.

Maxwell-Fyfe That is the English translation. I will show Dr. Stahmer the German.

Dr Stahmer Mr. President, I should like to point out, that the document bears no date and we do not know when and where it was drawn up,

Maxwell-Fyfe It is signed by the Defendant Raeder.

Dr Stahmer When and where was it drawn up? The signature of Raeder is unknown to me.

Maxwell-Fyfe The date is in Raeder's handwriting as is the signature; the 27th of July, I think it is 1945. Each page of the document is signed by the Defendant Raeder.

President Sir David, you said the defendant has put his character in issue through Bodenschatz?

Maxwell-Fyfe Your Lordship will remember he was asked by Doctor Stahmer: "Will you now tell me about the defendant's social relations?" And then he proceeded to give an account of his character and his kindness and other qualities at that time; and I notice that Doctor Stahmer has just included as an exhibit still further evidence as to character in the form of a statement by one Hermann Winter.

President Would it not have been appropriate, if the document was to have been put in evidence, to have put it to Bodenschatz, who was giving the evidence?

Maxwell-Fyfe But, My Lord, the rule is that if the defendant puts his character in issue, he is entitled to be cross-examined on his character and his general reputation, and of course it is permissible to call a witness to speak as to his general reputation.

Dr Stahmer May I make the following remark? I did not call Bodenschatz, neither did I question him as witness for Goering's character. I questioned him about certain facts and happenings from which Bodenschatz subsequently drew certain conclusions. In my opinion, all these questions should have been put to Bodenschatz when he was here. These statements could then have been used to prove that it was Bodenschatz who was not telling the truth, not that Goering had told an untruth. To prove this the document should have been used during Bodenschatz's interrogation. Then we would have been able to question Bodenschatz about it too.

Maxwell-Fyfe He may prefer that Bodenschatz be brought back and it be put to him, but I think I am entitled to put it to the defendant who called for the evidence as to his character and reputation.

President The Tribunal will adjourn.

[A recess was taken.]

President The Tribunal rules that at the present stage, this document cannot be used in cross-examination.

Maxwell-Fyfe If Your Honor please, I understand that Your

Lordship leaves open the question for further argument, whether it can be used for the Defendant Raeder in the witness box.

President Yes.

Maxwell-Fyfe I am much obliged.

[Turning to the witness.] Now, Witness, you said before the Tribunal adjourned, that Hitler, in your opinion, did not know about - broadly -- or was ignorant about, the question of concentration camps and the Jews. I would like you to look at Document Number D-736. That is an account of a discussion between the Fuehrer and the Hungarian Regent Horthy on the 17th of April 1943, and if you would look at Page 4, you will see the passage just after "Nuremberg and Furth."

Goering Just a moment. I should like to read through it very quickly to determine its authenticity.

Maxwell-Fyfe Certainly.

Goering Page 4.

Maxwell-Fyfe Page 4 -- Exhibit Number GB-283. You see, after the mention of Nuremberg and Furth, Hitler goes on:

"The Jews did not even possess organizational value. In spite of the fears which he, the Fuehrer, had heard repeatedly in Germany, everything continued to go its normal way without the Jews. Where the Jews were left to themselves, as for instance in Poland, the most terrible misery and decay prevailed. They are just pure parasites. In Poland, this state of affairs had been fundamentally cleared up. If the Jews there did not want to work they were shot. If they could not work, they had to perish. They had to be treated like tuberculosis bacilli, with which a healthy body may become infected.

"This was not cruel -- if one remembers that even innocent creatures of nature, such as hares and deer, have to be killed so that no harm is caused by them. Why should the beasts who wanted to bring us Bolshevism be more preserved? Nations which do not rid themselves of Jews perish. One of the most famous examples is the downfall of that people who were once so proud, the Persians, who now lead a pitiful existence as Armenians."

And would you look at Exhibit USSR-170, Document Number USSR-170, which is a conference which you had on the 6th of August 1942.

President Before you pass from this document, is there not a passage higher up that is important? It is about 10 lines down, I think, in the middle of the line ...

Maxwell-Fyfe Your Honor is correct.

"To Admiral Horthy's counter question as to what he should do with the Jews, now that they had been deprived of almost all possibility of earning their livelihood -- he could not kill them off -- the Reich Minister of Foreign Affairs declared that the Jews should be exterminated or taken to concentration camps. There was no other possibility."

Goering I do not know this document.

Maxwell-Fyfe Now, this is a conference which you had with a number of people, and on Page 143, if you will turn to it, you get on to the question of butter. If you will look where it says: "Reich Marshal Goering How much butter do you deliver? 30,000 tons?"

Do you see that?

Goering Yes.

Maxwell-Fyfe And then Lohse, who is in the conference, says, "Yes," and you say, "Do you also deliver to Wehrmacht units?" and then Lohse says, " I can answer that too. There are only a few Jews left alive. Tens of thousands have been disposed of, but I can tell you that the civilian population gets, on your orders, 15 percent less than the Germans." I call your attention to the statement that "there are only a few Jews left alive, tens of thousands have been disposed of." Do you still say, in the face of these two documents, that neither Hitler nor yourself knew that the Jews were being exterminated?

Goering I beg that the remarks be rightly read. They are quite incorrectly reproduced. May I read the original text? "Lohse:" -- thus not my remark, but the remark of Lohse -- "I can also answer that. The Jews are left only in small numbers. Thousands have gone." It does not say here that they were destroyed. From this remark you cannot conclude that they were killed. It could also mean that they had gone away -- they were removed. There is nothing here ...

Maxwell-Fyfe About the preceding remark, I suggest that you make quite clear what you meant by "there, are only a few Jews left alive, whereas tens of thousands have been disposed of."

Goering They were "still living there." That is how you should understand that.

Maxwell-Fyfe You heard what I read to you about Hitler, what he said to Horthy and what Ribbentrop said, that the Jews must be exterminated or taken to concentration camps. Hitler said the Jews must either work or be shot. That was in April 1943. Do you still say that neither Hitler nor you knew of this policy to exterminate the Jews?

Goering For the correctness of the document.

Maxwell-Fyfe Will you please answer my question. Do you still say neither Hitler nor you knew of the policy to exterminate the Jews?

Goering As far as Hitler is concerned, I have said I do not think so. As far as I am concerned, I have said that I did not know, even approximately, to what extent these things were taking place.

Maxwell-Fyfe You did not know to what degree, but you knew there was a policy that aimed at the extermination of the Jews?

Goering No, a policy of emigration, not liquidation of the Jews. I knew only that there had been isolated cases of such perpetrations.

Maxwell-Fyfe Thank you.

Goering's Final Statement
Morning Session – 31st August 1946

As part of the procedural rules of the Tribunal, before the judges retired to consider their verdicts, the defendants were able to make a final statement summarising their defence.

Goering's cross-examination had finished five months ago, on 22nd March, and he had sat through many days of evidence concerning his fellow defendants and the cases against various Nazi organisations. Perhaps he had taken the opportunity to consider deeply his part in the history of Nazism, or perhaps his attitudes were so fixed that no change was possible. Now he had a final opportunity to justify his participation in governing the Third Reich.

During the trial, Goering had been obliged to listen to the prosecution attacking his character and his integrity day after day. His own evidence from the witness stand had not softened those attacks, something which is very uncomfortable for any defendant but a normal part of the adversarial court system. No man enjoys having his failings illuminated in public but it must have been especially galling for some-one who, for so long, had held the highest authority and felt himself to be beyond reproach. In his final statement, Goering tried to reverse the impressions left on the Tribunal by the prosecution.

He gave no hint of remorse and although he did condemn the Nazis' mass murdering, he denied knowledge of it at the time. He did not explicitly accept any responsibility for the dark events of the Second World War, and instead threw himself onto the judgement of history and the German people.

President Article 24 D (j) provides that each defendant may make a statement to the Tribunal. I therefore now can upon the defendants who wish--whether they wish to make statements. Defendant Hermann Wilhelm Goering.

Goering The prosecution, in the final speeches, has treated the defendants and their testimony as completely worthless. The statements made under oath by the defendants were accepted as absolutely true when they could serve to support the Indictment, but conversely the statements were characterized as perjury when they refuted the Indictment. That is very elementary, but it is not a convincing basis for demonstration of proof.

The prosecution uses the fact that I was the second man of the State as proof that I must have known everything that happened. But it does not present any documentary or other convincing proof in cases where I have denied under oath that I knew about certain things, much less desired them. Therefore, it is only an allegation and a conjecture when the prosecution says, "Who should have known that if not Goering, who was the successor of the Fuehrer?"

Repeatedly we have heard here how the worst crimes were veiled with the most secrecy. I wish to state expressly that I condemn these terrible mass murders to the utmost, and cannot understand them in the least. But I should like to state clearly once more before the High Tribunal, that I have never decreed the murder of a single individual at any time, and neither did I decree any other atrocities or tolerate them, while I had the power and the knowledge to prevent them.

The new allegation presented by Mr. Dodd in his final speech, that I had ordered Heydrich to kill the Jews, lacks every proof and is not true either. There is not a single order signed by me or signed on my behalf that enemy fliers should be shot or turned over to the SD. And not a single case has been established where units of my Luftwaffe carried out things like that.

The prosecution has repeatedly submitted some documents which contain alleged statements, reported and written down at third and fourth hand, without my having previously seen these statements in order to correct erroneous ideas or to preclude misunderstandings.

How easily completely distorted reports can arise from third hand notes is also proven, among other things, by the stenographic transcript of these court sessions, which often needed correction when checked.

The prosecution brings forward individual statements over a period of 25 years, which were made under completely different circumstances and without any consequences arising from them at the time, and quotes them as proof of intent and guilt, statements which can easily be made in the excitement of the moment and of the atmosphere that prevailed at the time. There is probably not one leading personage on the opposing side who did not speak or write similarly in the course of a quarter of a century.

Out of all the happenings of these 25 years, from conferences, speeches, laws, actions, and decisions, the prosecution proves that everything was desired and intended from the beginning according to a deliberate sequence and an unbroken connection. This is an erroneous conception which is entirely devoid of logic, and which will be rectified some day by history, after the proceedings here have proved the incorrectness of these allegations.

Mr. Jackson in his final speech points, out the fact that the signatory states are still in a state of war with Germany, and that because of the unconditional surrender merely a state of truce prevails now. Now, international law is uniform. The same must apply to both sides. Therefore, if everything which is being done in Germany today on the part of the occupying powers is admissible under international law, then German was formerly in the same position, at least as regards France, Holland, Belgium, Norway, Yugoslavia and Greece.

If today the Geneva Convention no longer has any validity so far as Germans are concerned, if today in all parts of Germany industry is being dismantled and other great assets in all spheres can be carried away to the other states, if today the property of millions of Germans is being confiscated and many other serious infringements on freedom and property are taking place, then measures such as those taken by Germany in the countries mentioned above cannot have been criminal according to international law either.

Mr. Jackson stated further that one cannot accuse and punish a state, but rather that one must hold the leaders responsible. One seems to forget that Germany was a sovereign state, and that her legislation within the German nation was not subject to the jurisdiction of foreign countries. No state ever gave notice to the Reich at the proper time, pointing out that any activity for National Socialism would be made subject to punishment and persecution. On the other hand, if we, the leaders as individuals, are called to account and condemned--very well; but you cannot punish the German people at the same time.

The German people placed their trust in the Fuehrer, and under his authoritarian government they had no influence on events. Without knowledge of the grave crimes which have become known today, the people, loyal, self-sacrificing, and courageous, fought and suffered through the life-and-death struggle which had broken out against their will. The German people are free of guilt.

I did not want a war, nor did I bring it about. I did everything to prevent it by negotiations. After it had broken out, I did everything to assure victory. Since the three greatest powers on earth, together with many other nations, were fighting against us, we finally succumbed to their tremendous superiority.

I stand up for the things that I have done, but I deny most emphatically that my actions were dictated by the desire to subjugate foreign peoples by wars, to murder them, to rob them, or to enslave them, or to commit atrocities or crimes.

The only motive which guided me was my ardent love for my people, its happiness, its freedom, and its life. And for this I call on the Almighty and my German people to witness.

Verdict and Sentence
Morning Session – 1ˢᵗ October 1946

On the morning of 1ˢᵗ October 1946, the Tribunal convened to announce its verdicts on all the defendants.

The drafting of the judgement had begun as far back as April, as the judges struggled to define the international laws and principles behind their decisions. The discussions, between eight highly respected individuals from four different legal systems, were always difficult. In particular, the charge of conspiracy returned with a vengeance and in the end the decision was taken to limit this charge only to the waging of aggressive war.

The judges had hoped to give unanimous verdicts on 23ʳᵈ September, but as that day neared, they realised they would not be ready and decided on a further week's discussions.

For the defendants, who had been held for over a year, this extra week must have been agonising. They had always been under a suicide watch but now this was intensified. The prison authorities assigned a new psychiatrist, Dr Dunn, to continuously monitor their mental condition. Dunn estimated that Goering, while not at all depressed, might take any chance to go down fighting and for that reason was a suicide risk. Apart from that he seemed strong and determined, and Dunn predicted he would 'face his sentence bolstered by his own egocentricity, bravado and showmanship'.

The morning session of 1ˢᵗ October would be the last time the defendants sat together in the dock. The reading of the verdicts against individuals was shared between the judges. They were read in the order of the indictment with the President, Sir Geoffrey Lawrence, reading the verdict found against Goering.

President Article 26 of the Charter provides that the Judgment of the Tribunal as to the guilt or innocence of any defendant shall give the reasons on which it is based.

The Tribunal will now state those reasons in declaring its judgment on such guilt or innocence.

Goering

Goering is indicted on all four Counts. The evidence shows that, after Hitler, he was the most prominent man in the Nazi regime. He was Commander-in-Chief of the Luftwaffe, Plenipotentiary for the Four Year Plan, and had tremendous influence with Hitler, at least until 1943, when their relationship deteriorated, ending in his arrest in 1945. He testified that Hitler kept him informed of all important military and political problems.

Crimes against Peace

From the moment he joined the Party in 1922 and took command of the street-fighting organization, the SA, Goering was the adviser, the active agent of Hitler, and one of the prime leaders of the Nazi movement. As Hitler's political deputy he was largely instrumental in bringing the National Socialists to power in 1933 and was charged with consolidating this power and expanding German armed might.

He developed the Gestapo and created the first concentration camps, relinquishing them to Himmler in 1934, conducted the Roehm purge in that year, and engineered the sordid proceedings which resulted in the removal of Von Blomberg and Von Fritsch from the Army. In 1936 he became Plenipotentiary of the Four Year Plan and in theory and in practice was the economic dictator of the Reich. Shortly after the Pact of Munich, he announced that he would embark on a five-fold expansion of the Luftwaffe and speed up rearmament with emphasis on offensive weapons.

Goering was one of the five important leaders present at the Hossbach conference of 5 November 1937, and he attended the other important conferences already discussed in this Judgment. In the Austrian Anschluss he was indeed the central figure, the ringleader. He said in court: "I must take 100 percent responsibility... I even overruled objections by the Fuehrer and brought everything to its final development." In the seizure of the Sudetenland, he played his role as Luftwaffe chief by planning an air offensive which proved unnecessary, and his role as a politician by lulling the Czechs with false promises of friendship. The night before the invasion of Czechoslovakia and the absorption of Bohemia and Moravia, at a conference with Hitler and President Hacha, he threatened to bomb Prague if Hacha did not submit. This threat he admitted in his testimony.

Goering attended the Reich Chancellery meeting of 23 May 1939, when Hitler told his military leaders "there is, therefore, no question of sparing Poland," and was present at the Obersalzberg briefing of 22 August 1939. And the evidence shows he was active in the diplomatic manoeuvres which followed. With Hitler's connivance, he used the Swedish businessman, Dahlerus, as a go-between to the British, as described by Dahlerus to this Tribunal, to try to prevent the British Government from keeping its guarantee to the Poles.

He commanded the Luftwaffe in the attack on Poland and throughout the aggressive wars which followed.

Even if he opposed Hitler's plans against Norway and the Soviet Union, as he alleged, it is clear that he did so only for strategic reasons; once Hitler had decided the issue, he followed him without hesitation. He made it clear in his testimony that these differences were never ideological or legal.

He was "in a rage" about the invasion of Norway, but only because he had not received sufficient warning to prepare the Luftwaffe offensive. He admitted he approved of the attack: "My attitude was perfectly positive." He was active in preparing and executing the Yugoslavian and Greek campaigns and testified that "Plan Marita", the attack on Greece, had been prepared long beforehand. The Soviet Union he regarded as the "most threatening menace to Germany," but said there was no immediate military necessity for the attack. Indeed, his only objection to the war of aggression against the U.S.S.R. was its timing; he wished for strategic reasons to delay until Britain was conquered. He testified: "My point of view was decided by political and military reasons only."

After his own admissions to this Tribunal, from the positions which he held, the conferences he attended, and the public words he uttered, there can remain no doubt that Goering was the moving force for aggressive war second only to Hitler. He was the planner and prime mover in the military and diplomatic preparation for war which Germany pursued.

War Crimes and Crimes against Humanity

The record is filled with Goering's admissions of his complicity in the use of slave labor. "We did use this labor for security reasons so that they would not be active in their own country and would not work against us. On the other hand, they served to help in the economic war." And again: "Workers were forced to come to the Reich. That is something I have not denied." The man who spoke these words was Plenipotentiary for the Four Year Plan charged with the recruitment and allocation of manpower. As Luftwaffe Commander-in-Chief he demanded from Himmler more slave laborers for his underground aircraft factories: "That I requested inmates of concentration camps for the armament of the Luftwaffe is correct and it is to be taken as a matter of course."

As plenipotentiary, Goering signed a directive concerning the treatment of Polish workers in Germany and implemented it by regulations of the SD, including "special treatment." He issued directives to use Soviet and French prisoners of war in the armament industry; he spoke of seizing Poles and Dutch and making them prisoners of war if necessary, and using them for work. He agrees Russian prisoners of war were used to man anti-aircraft batteries.

As plenipotentiary, Goering was the active authority in the spoliation of conquered territory. He made plans for the spoliation of Soviet territory long before the war on the Soviet Union. Two months prior to the invasion of the Soviet Union, Hitler gave Goering the overall direction for the economic administration in the territory. Goering set up an economic staff for this function. As Reich Marshal of the Greater German Reich, "the orders of the Reich Marshal cover all economic fields, including nutrition and agriculture." His so-called "Green" folder, printed by the Wehrmacht, set up an "Economic Executive Staff East." This directive contemplated plundering and abandonment of all industry in the food deficit regions and, from the food surplus regions, a diversion of food to German needs. Goering claims its purposes have been misunderstood, but admits "that as a matter of course and a matter of duty we would have used Russia for our purposes" when conquered.

And he participated in the conference of 16 July when Hitler said the National Socialists had no intention of ever leaving the occupied countries, and that "all necessary measures - shooting, resettling, *et cetera--*" should be taken.

Goering persecuted the Jews, particularly after the November 1938 riots, and not only in Germany, where he raised the billion-mark fine as stated elsewhere, but in the conquered territories as well. His own utterances then and his testimony now shows this interest was primarily economic-how to get their property and how to force them out of the economic life of Europe. As these countries fell before the German Army, he extended the Reich anti-Jewish laws to them; the *Reichsgesetzblatt* for 1939, 1940, and 1941 contains several anti-Jewish decrees signed by Goering. Although their extermination was in Himmler's hands, Goering was far from disinterested or inactive, despite his protestations in the witness box. By decree of 31 July 1941 he directed Himmler and Heydrich to "bring about a complete solution of the Jewish question in the German sphere of influence in Europe."

There is nothing to be said in mitigation. For Goering was often, indeed almost always, the moving force, second only to his leader. He was the leading war aggressor, both as political and as military leader; he was the director of the slave labor program and the creator of the oppressive program against the Jews and other races, at home and abroad. All of these crimes he has frankly admitted.

On some specific cases there may be conflict of testimony, but in terms of the broad outline his own admissions are more than sufficiently wide to be conclusive of his guilt. His guilt is unique in its enormity. The record discloses no excuses for this man.

Conclusion

The Tribunal finds the Defendant Goering guilty on all four Counts of the Indictment.

Afternoon Session – 1st October 1946

The afternoon session was devoted to sentencing. The culmination of the trial inevitably brought sentences of death for some of the defendants and in order to treat the prisoners humanely, cameras were banned from the courtroom and the flood lights switched off.

The defendants were brought in one by one and stood alone in the dock to hear their sentences. Goering, at the head of the indictment, was brought in first between two military policemen. He wore his Luftwaffe uniform, now fitting very loosely because of the weight he had lost during captivity. He stood to attention as Sir Geoffrey Lawrence began to read, but immediately stopped the proceeding because his headphones were not working. A heart-stopping few minutes followed while the headphones were replaced, and replaced again, until Goering signaled that he could hear.

President In accordance with Article 27 of the Charter, the International Military Tribunal will now pronounce the sentences on the defendants convicted on this Indictment:

Defendant Hermann Wilhelm Goering, on the Counts of the Indictment on which you have been convicted, the International Military Tribunal sentences you to death by hanging.

At the end of sentencing, the defendants were told that they could appeal to the mercy of the Allied Control Council. All defendants appealed, and Goering appealed to be shot rather than face hanging like a common criminal. The Council decided not to amend the Tribunal's decisions.

Goering was immediately taken to his cell, along with the ten other men sentenced to hang. A date for the executions was not announced and, after they had taken care of their final business, the prisoners waited in limbo. The executions were carried out on the night of 15th to 16th October, but Goering did not hang.

In a final act of defiance, at about quarter to eleven that night, Goering bit into a capsule of cyanide and died in minutes.

From the start of the trail, he knew he could not escape a death sentence but, armed with no more than force of personality, he had led a mixed group of defendants through their long trial. None of them had broken down and confessed to their crimes. None of them had disgraced Germany by behaving in an unmanly fashion. Although there had been some criticism of Hitler, they had all, in the end, denied collective and individual guilt.

That achieved, Goering chose to cheat the hangman and die by his own hand.

Epilogue – the Final Statement of Albert Speer

This account has focussed on Goering because he was by far the most important defendant at Nuremberg. He stood at the centre of the Third Reich and was complicit in its criminal history. He stood out amongst the other defendants by his quick-witted intelligence and the sheer charisma built up through years of near absolute power.

No-one could better symbolise the rottenness of the Nazi regime, but I have left the last word to another defendant, Albert Speer.

Speer was not a military man but an architect. He was attracted to Hitler and his power, and was the nearest thing to a friend that Hitler had. Speer was an extremely efficient technocrat and finished the war as Minister for Armaments and Munitions with fourteen million people working for him, both Germans and forced labour.

By character, Speer was very reserved and found intimacy and openness difficult. His family life, both as a husband and a father, seems impossibly cold to a modern reader.

He thought clearly and analytically, and that is what took him to the top of the Third Reich, and allowed him to survive the Nuremberg trial when many thought he should have been hanged. The final words of his defence case come from an educated man who, for a period, was one of the most powerful men in the world. For all his time at the summit of power, he had been scrambling to defend Germany, and to fend off the results of Hitler's crazy commitment to fight until the bitter end. Since his arrest over a year ago, he had had plenty of time to consider the great and terrible events he had been part of, and to come to some conclusions.

Alone among the defendants, he did not devote his final statement to exculpation. Instead he gave his twenty minutes to condemning Hitler and his dictatorship, and warning the world of the danger of future wars. His words make a fitting ending for this book.

Saturday, 31 August 1946

President I call on the Defendant Albert Speer.

Speer Mr. President, may it please the Tribunal: Hitler and the collapse of his system have brought a time of tremendous suffering upon the German people. The useless continuation of this war and the unnecessary destruction make the work of reconstruction more difficult. Privation and misery have come to the German people. After this trial, the German people will despise and condemn Hitler as the proven author of its misfortune. But the world will learn from these happenings not only to hate dictatorship as a form of government, but to fear it.

Hitler's dictatorship differed in one fundamental point from all its predecessors in history. His was the first dictatorship in the present period of modern technical development, a dictatorship which made complete use of all technical means in a perfect manner for the domination of its own nation.

Through technical devices such as radio and loudspeaker, 80 million people were deprived of independent thought. It was thereby possible to subject them to the will of one man. The telephone, teletype, and radio made it possible, for instance, for orders from the highest sources to be transmitted directly to the lowest-ranking units, where, because of the high authority, they were carried out without criticism. Another result was that numerous offices and headquarters were directly attached to the supreme leadership, from which they received their sinister orders directly. Also, one of the results was a far-reaching supervision of the citizen of the state and the maintenance of a high degree of secrecy for criminal events.

Perhaps to the outsider this machinery of the state may appear like the lines of a telephone exchange - apparently without system. But like the latter, it could be served and dominated by one single will.

Earlier dictators during their work of leadership needed highly qualified assistants, even at the lowest level, men who could think and act independently. The totalitarian system in the period of modern technical development can dispense with them; the means of communication alone make it possible to mechanize the subordinate leadership. As a result of this there arises a new type: the uncritical recipient of orders.

. We had only reached the beginning of the development. The nightmare of many a man that one day nations could be dominated by technical means was all but realized in Hitler's totalitarian system.

Today the danger of being terrorized by technocracy threatens every country in the world. In modern dictatorship this appears to me inevitable. Therefore, the more technical the world becomes, the more necessary is the promotion of individual freedom and the individual's awareness of himself as a counterbalance.

Hitler not only took advantage of technical developments to dominate his own people - he almost succeeded, by means of his technical lead, in subjugating the whole of Europe. It was merely due to a few fundamental shortcomings of organization such as are typical in a dictatorship because of the absence of criticism, that he did not have twice as many tanks, aircraft, and submarines before 1942.

But, if a modern industrial state utilizes its intelligence, its science, its technical developments, and its production for a number of years in order to gain a lead in the sphere of armament, then even with a sparing use of its manpower it can, because of its technical superiority, completely overtake and conquer the world, if other nations should employ their technical abilities during that same period on behalf of the cultural progress of humanity.

The more technical the world becomes, the greater this danger will be, and the more serious will be an established lead in the technical means of warfare.

This war ended with remote-controlled rockets, aircraft travelling at the speed of sound, new types of submarines, torpedoes which find their own target, with atom bombs, and with the prospect of a horrible kind of chemical warfare.

Of necessity, the next war will be overshadowed by these new destructive inventions of the human mind.

In 5 or 10 years the technique of warfare will make it possible to fire rockets from continent to continent with uncanny precision. By atomic power it can destroy one million people in the center of New York in a matter of seconds with a rocket operated, perhaps, by only 10 men, invisible, without previous warning, faster than sound, by day and by night. Science is able to spread pestilence among human beings and animals and to destroy crops by insect warfare. Chemistry has developed terrible weapons with which it can inflict unspeakable suffering upon helpless human beings.

Will there ever again be a nation which will use the technical discoveries of this war for the preparation of a new war, while the rest of the world is employing the technical progress of this war for the benefit of humanity, thus attempting to create a slight compensation for its horrors? As a former minister of a highly developed armament system, it is my last duty to say the following:

A new large-scale war will end with the destruction of human culture and civilization. Nothing can prevent unconfined engineering and science from completing the work of destroying human beings, which it has begun in so dreadful a way in this war.

Therefore this trial must contribute towards preventing such degenerate wars in the future, and towards establishing rules whereby human beings can live together.

Of what importance is my own fate, after everything that has happened, in comparison with this high goal?

During the past centuries the German people have contributed much towards the creation of human civilization. Often they have made these contributions in times when they were just as powerless and helpless as they are today. Worth-while human beings will not let themselves be driven to despair. They will create new and lasting values, and under the tremendous pressure brought to bear upon everyone today these new works will be of particular greatness.

But if the German people create new cultural values in the unavoidable times of their poverty and weakness, and at the same time in the period of their reconstruction, then they will have in that way made the most valuable contribution to world events which they could make in their position.

It is not the battles of war alone which shape the history of humanity, but also, in a higher sense, the cultural achievements which one day will become the common property of all humanity. A nation which believes in its future will never perish. May God protect Germany and the culture of the West.

More books by Jacqueline George can be found at
www.jacquelinegeorgewriter.com

www.ingramcontent.com/pod-product-compliance
Lightning Source LLC
LaVergne TN
LVHW031629070426
835507LV00024B/3401